THE PALESTINIANS IN PERSPECTIVE

IMPLICATIONS FOR MIDEAST PEACE AND U.S. POLICY

GEORGE E. GRUEN

YEHOSHAFAT HARKABI

DANIEL J. ELAZAR

GALIA GOLAN

RITA E. HAUSER

Edited by
GEORGE E. GRUEN

INSTITUTE OF HUMAN RELATIONS PRESS
The American Jewish Committee
165 East 56th Street, New York, N.Y. 10022

This publication was made possible through the generosity of the Henry and Marilyn Taub Foundation. Thanks are due also to Robert Goldmann, who played a key role in initiating this project.

CONTENTS

PREFACE

Those who wish to understand what is going on in the Middle East today confront an anomaly. The region is swamped in a series of conflicts, extending from the Western Sahara to the Persian Gulf: Arabs against Israel, oil producers against oil consumers, the Soviet Union against the West, Iraq against Iran, Arabs against Arabs, Muslims against Muslims. Many of the regimes in the area are torn by internal struggle and secessionist pressures. Militant Muslim fundamentalism has led to the death of Anwar Sadat, as well as to uprisings against Hafez al-Assad in Syria, and has threatened to undermine both the conservative Saudi monarchy and the secular Turkish republic. In Lebanon and Iran, civil strife approaches the anarchic state well described by Hobbes — the war of all against all.

Yet one conflict, the Arab-Israeli conflict, seems to dominate the media and even the discussion of public policy to such a disproportionate degree that it overshadows all the other confrontations in the region. This conflict is seen more and more in terms of a single issue: resolving the problem of the Palestinian Arabs and redressing their grievances.

The end of the first phase of the Camp David peace process, concluding in Israel's final withdrawal from the Sinai on April 25, 1982, has thrown the issue into even sharper focus. Palestinian grievances, especially as presented by the Palestine Liberation Organization, are aired at the United Nations more frequently than any other topic. Organizations such as the Socialist International see Palestinian self-determination as a key element in a Western approach to the Third World. The subject was one cause of the painful rift in U.S.-European relations which culminated in the Venice Declaration, a rift which has somewhat narrowed, but still remains a potential source of discord. In Washington, important officials are known to believe that the Palestinian problem must be resolved if the internal stability of the entire Middle East and oil-producing Gulf states is to be assured. Countries actively courted as allies by the United States, such as Saudi Arabia, vigorously press for such resolution. Moreover, it is asserted that U.S. strategy for recruiting an anti-Soviet coalition among the Muslim states cannot succeed unless the United States makes "progress" on the Palestinian issue.

Is the centrality accorded to the Palestinian grievances by the media, by international organizations and by U.S. policy makers justified in the face of recent events and Middle East history?

In recent years, what used to be unthinkable has not only been thought but translated into fact: Egypt has made peace with Israel — even though both sides recognize that the Palestinian problem is not yet resolved. And the most grievous injuries inflicted on American interests in the Persian Gulf — the Iranian revolution, the doubling of OPEC's oil prices in 1979 (prior to the present glut and slight drop), the Soviet invasion of Afghanistan — were neither caused, nor critically influenced, by the course of the Arab-Israeli conflict or by the status of the Palestinians. The threat to the stability of the Gulf states by a Khomeini, or the shock to Saudi Arabia from the takeover of the Grand Mosque by a group of religious fanatics critical of Saudi corruption resulted from internal matters and not from the Palestinian question.

Clearly, an understanding of the relative weight and real significance of the Palestinian grievances as they affect U.S. national security interests is necessary for the formulation of an appropriate American policy on the Middle East and for determining the nature of U.S. relations with Israel. If as many argue, the rapid resolution of those grievances in a manner satisfactory to Palestinian spokesmen — especially the PLO — is a fundamental requirement for American security, then obviously everything should be done to reach such a settlement at once, even over Israeli protests. If such is not the case, however, if a one-sided settlement of Palestinian grievances would not materially reduce the risks to American interests but might even increase them, then too the United States should act accordingly.

The purpose of this volume is twofold:

— It seeks, first, to put Palestinian grievances in proper proportion — in relation to the Arab-Israeli conflict, to the Arab states themselves, to the Soviet-American rivalry, and to the efforts of the United States and the United Nations to achieve a just and lasting resolution of the problem. This general background and broad context is provided in Part I, which consists of two essays by Dr. George E. Gruen, on Palestine as an arena for international power struggles and on the Palestinians as a focus of inter-Arab rivalry.

— Secondly, it explores the dimensions of the Palestinian issue from several perspectives: the attitudes of the Palestinians themselves (especially of the PLO and its diverse factions), the varying Israeli responses, Moscow's use of the issue to advance its own foreign policy goals, the evolution of the American position and the implications for U.S. policy. Specialized essays on these topics by Professors Yehoshafat Harkabi, Daniel J. Elazar, Galia Golan and Dr. Rita E. Hauser make up Part II of the volume. Obviously, the opinions expressed are those of the authors and not necessarily those of the American Jewish Committee.

That the United States needs to pay attention to the Palestinians — both as a humanitarian problem and as a political issue — is evident. This is not the same, however, as permitting the agenda of United States policy vis-à-vis the Middle East to be dominated by Palestinian grievances. Such a simplistic approach would do a disservice to American interests by distorting the complex realities of the region. In formulating policy, our nation must also weigh the many other matters that are at least as crucial, it not decisive, to American security and to peace in the Middle East.

BERTRAM H. GOLD
Executive Vice President

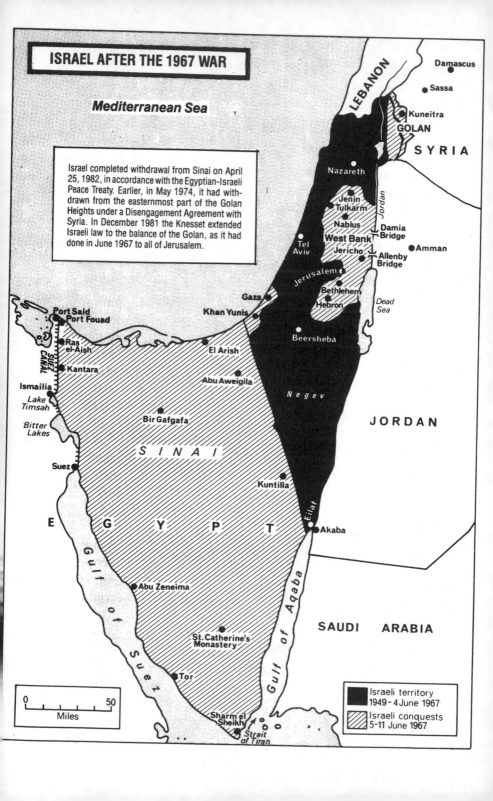

ISRAEL AFTER THE 1967 WAR

Mediterranean Sea

Israel completed withdrawal from Sinai on April 25, 1982, in accordance with the Egyptian-Israeli Peace Treaty. Earlier, in May 1974, it had withdrawn from the easternmost part of the Golan Heights under a Disengagement Agreement with Syria. In December 1981 the Knesset extended Israeli law to the balance of the Golan, as it had done in June 1967 to all of Jerusalem.

LEBANON

Damascus

Sassa

Kuneitra
GOLAN

SYRIA

Nazareth

Jenin
Tulkarm

Nablus

Damia
Bridge

West Bank

Tel
Aviv

Jericho

Amman

Allenby
Bridge

Jerusalem

Bethlehem

Gaza

Hebron

Dead
Sea

Khan Yunis

Beersheba

El Arish

Abu Aweigila

Negev

JORDAN

Port Said
Port Fouad

Ras
el-Aish

Kantara

Ismailia
Lake
Timsah

Bitter
Lakes

Bir Gafgafa

S I N A I

Suez

Kuntilla

E   G   Y   P   T

Eilat
Akaba

Abu Zeneima

Gulf of Aqaba

SAUDI   ARABIA

Gulf of Suez

St. Catherine's
Monastery

Tor

0   50
Miles

Sharm el
Sheikh

Strait
of Tiran

SUEZ CANAL

■ Israeli territory
1949 – 4 June 1967

▨ Israeli conquests
5-11 June 1967

PART ONE: THE OVERVIEW

George E. Gruen

THE PALESTINIAN QUESTION
IN INTERNATIONAL POLITICS

Since biblical times, the region known as Palestine — *Falastin* in Arabic and *Eretz Israel* in Hebrew — has been a major arena for international power struggles. Throughout history, empires fought each other for control of this strategic piece of territory on the eastern Mediterranean, which links Asia and Africa by land and borders the sea lanes from the Mediterranean to the Red Sea. When the area was not being ravaged by invading armies, it served as an important transit route for caravans. From the Holy Land in which monotheism originated, the ideas of social justice proclaimed in the Bible were propagated by Judaism, Christianity and Islam, and profoundly affected world civilization.

The modern interest in Palestine dates from the breakup of the Ottoman Empire during World War I. Palestine and the outlying Arab countries had been under Turkish rule for four centuries. Long before, in anticipation of the demise of "the Sick Man of Europe," Britain, France and Russia began to assert their influence in the region and vied with one another for their share of the spoils (at the last moment, the Russian Revolution prevented Moscow from realizing its objectives).

Under the influence of Wilson's principle of self-determination, Britain and France did not simply divide the area into spheres of influence, but also provided for eventual independence of the Arab territories of the region. France obtained mandates over Syria and Lebanon, and gained control of Algeria, Tunisia and Morocco. Britain, which had played a preeminent role in Egypt since 1882 and extended the Egyptian frontier in 1906 to include the Sinai, insisted on securing the mandates for Palestine and Iraq. This

1

served the useful geostrategic purpose of keeping its rival imperial power, France, as far away as possible from the Suez Canal, the British Empire's lifeline to India. Palestine, including Transjordan, was linked by a broad corridor across the desert to Iraq, to insure that the projected oil pipeline to the Mediterranean would also remain under British control.

While World War I raged, the British had entered into negotiations with the Hashemite leader, Sherif Hussein of Mecca. They promised him that if he joined them in ousting the Turks, they would place him at the head of an independent Arab empire. Palestine was to be excluded from this empire, since the British had promised to establish a Jewish national home there. Hussein was prepared at one point to conclude a treaty of cooperation with Chaim Weizmann, the Zionist leader, but it never came to fruition, in large measure because France's insistence on ruling Syria led the French to expel Faisal, Hussein's son, from Damascus, which Hussein had planned to make the capital of his Arab empire. The British eventually installed Faisal as King of Iraq, while the resurgent Saudi family under Abdel Aziz Ibn Saud expelled the Hashemites from the Arabian peninsula.

Palestine Under British Mandate

Unlike other mandates awarded by the League of Nations, the Mandate for Palestine did not provide for future Arab independence. While the local population was to share in self-governing institutions, the main objective of the British Mandatory Administration, according to the Council of the League of Nations, was to implement the British Government's support of "Jewish Zionist aspirations" contained in the November 1917 Balfour Declaration:

> His Majesty's Government view with favour the establishment in Palestine of a national home for the Jewish people and will use their best endeavours to facilitate the achievement of this object...

In the preamble to the Mandatory Agreement of July 24, 1922, the League of Nations Council endorsed the Balfour Declaration and noted that recognition had been given thereby "to the historical connexion of the Jewish people with Palestine and to the grounds for reconstituting their national home in that country."[1] The Mandatory Administration was called upon to facilitate Jewish immigration and land settlement, and to work with the Zionist Organization to elicit the support of Jews around the world for the Jewish national home.

Although isolationist sentiment in America prevented the United States from joining the League of Nations, the text of the Mandate agreement was incorporated in the Anglo-American Convention of 1924. Thus the U.S. Senate gave formal approval to President Wilson's earlier endorsement of the Balfour Declaration (U.S. Treaty Series, No. 728).

The text of the Balfour Declaration contained two qualifications regarding the implementation of the Jewish national home, namely, "that nothing shall be done which may prejudice the civil and religious rights of existing non-Jewish communities in Palestine, or the rights and political status enjoyed by Jews in any other country." From the very beginning, the British Administration was subjected to conflicting demands as it sought to reconcile the Zionist objective ultimately to establish a sovereign Jewish state in Palestine with mounting Arab opposition to any solution other than an independent Arab state in all of Palestine.

The British gradually whittled down their commitment to the Jews under the Balfour Declaration. Already in 1922, Winston Churchill, then British Colonial Secretary, won the League Council's approval to "postpone or withhold" application of the Jewish national home provisions in that section of the Palestine mandate lying east of the Jordan River. This territory, which comprises more than three-fourths of the original Palestine mandate, was handed over to Abdullah, another son of the Hashemite family. Originally bearing the title of Emir, Abdullah became King in 1946 when Transjordan declared its independence. Britain never asked the United Nations, the League's successor, to approve this unilateral decision to create an independent Arab state in the major portion of historic Palestine. Thus, when the "Palestine Question" was placed by Britain on the UN agenda in May 1947, the discussion was limited to the disposition of the territory on the West Bank of the Jordan River.[2]

3

The General Assembly established a UN Special Committee On Palestine (UNSCOP), composed of neutral states with no vested interests in the region. These found that the conflicting aspirations to independence of the Arabs and the Jews made a unitary solution impractical. Indeed, bitterness and strife between the two communities had sharpened over the years. Jewish pressure for increasing immigration became acute as persecution of Jews in Nazi Germany increased after 1932. Arab opposition to Jewish immigration had erupted into violent demonstrations in 1921, 1929 and 1936 to 1939. A British proposal to partition the country in 1936 was totally rejected by the Arabs. Moderate Arabs who seemed prepared to allow a minuscule Jewish state in part of Palestine were systematically assassinated by supporters of the Mufti, who dominated the Arab Higher Committee. As war clouds gathered over Europe, the British, eager to win Arab world support, adopted a White Paper in 1939 severely restricting Jewish immigration and land purchase in Palestine.

As news of the genocide of the Jewish communities of Nazi-occupied Europe reached the Jews of Palestine, they embarked on intensified efforts at "illegal" immigration to rescue the survivors. At the same time, some Jewish groups used terrorist tactics against British officials in Palestine, in a desperate attempt to bring about a change in Britain's policy and achieve independence. When UNSCOP investigated the situation, it found that guerrilla warfare between Arab and Jewish groups in Palestine had mounted. Over Arab objections, UNSCOP also visited Displaced Persons camps in Europe, where, two years after the end of the war, more than 225,000 Jewish survivors were still languishing, most of them desiring to go to Palestine. In addition, thousands of "illegal" immigrants intercepted by British gunboats were being held in internment camps in Cyprus.

UNSCOP recommended the termination of the Mandate. Because of the irreconcilable differences between Arabs and Jews, it stipulated also that Palestine be partitioned into two independent states, linked by an economic union and with free access by both to an international enclave containing Jerusalem and Bethlehem. On November 29, 1947, a two-thirds majority of the UN General Assembly approved the partition proposal.

This broad international consensus included the United States and the democracies of the Western European continent, the Soviet Union and the Eastern European bloc, Latin America, Australia and New Zealand. The limited opposition consisted of the six Arab members, four states containing Muslim majorities, Cuba, Greece and India. Britain abstained.

Soviet and American Support for Partition

Soviet support for the UN Partition Plan came as a major surprise in view of Moscow's previous record of opposition to the Zionist movement. Most observers believe that the shift was not due to any belated conversion of Stalin to Herzl's ideology, but that it reflected Moscow's pragmatic judgment that any step which hastened British evacuation from Palestine would strengthen the Soviet position in the region.

British Foreign Ministry officials, who opposed the creation of an independent Jewish state, spread rumors that many of the Jewish displaced persons seeking to enter Palestine were Communists, and that the Jewish state, many of whose leaders were socialists of East-European origin, would turn into a Soviet satellite. The British did not wish to incur the wrath of the Arab and Islamic world, which threatened violent opposition to a Jewish state.

Similar fears were voiced by American career diplomats in the State Department and the Pentagon. They tended to follow the British lead in policy relating to the Middle East, which had long been an area of British predominance, while the American involvement up to this time had been largely limited to missionary, educational, philanthropic and commercial interests. But President Truman overruled his State Department Arabists and used American diplomatic influence to gain votes for partition.

Washington and Moscow
Pursue Contrary Objectives

As bitter fighting broke out between the Palestinian Arab and Jewish communities, and Britain did little to maintain order, the Soviet Union proposed an international United Nations force, with Soviet and American participation, to restore order in Palestine.

The problem became even more acute on May 15, 1948. After the British withdrew and Israel proclaimed its independence, the regular armies of the neighboring Arab states and Iraq entered the conflict.

The United States faced a dilemma. Its own armed forces had been rapidly demobilized after the end of World War II. The growing threat posed by Soviet encroachments on Eastern Europe — the takeover of East Germany, Poland, Hungary, Bulgaria, Rumania and Czechoslovakia, compounded by Soviet territorial demands on Turkey and support for Communists in the civil war in Greece — stretched the existing American forces in Europe to a maximum. There were none to spare to police Palestine. Moreover, Truman agreed with his defense advisers that it was not in the American interest to support the creation of a UN armed force which would legitimize Soviet military presence in the Middle East. Consequently, the UN was limited to calling upon the parties to end the fighting and to providing mediation services. Only after Israel had routed the Arab armies in battle did the four neighboring Arab states finally consent, in 1949, to conclude armistice agreements under UN Mediator Ralph Bunche, an American political scientist.

The Palestinians were the main victims of their uncompromising leadership and of the aggressive policies of the neighboring Arab states. Egypt placed the Gaza Strip under its military administration, and Jordan incorporated what was left of the West Bank into the Hashemite Kingdom. Although the Jordanian action was approved by a council of Palestinian notables meeting in Jericho, most of the other Arab states refused to recognize its legitimacy. In the international community, only Britain and Pakistan formally accepted Jordan's sovereignty over the West Bank.

The UN proved totally ineffective in assuring the peace and security of Jerusalem as an open city under UN jurisdiction. In fact, the city became the scene of fierce fighting in 1948, after which parts of Jerusalem were split between the contenders. Jordan gained control of the Old City and expelled its Jewish residents, whereas Israel retained the new city. As a result of the fighting, Israel also increased the territory under its jurisdiction over what it had been allotted in the partition plan of 1947.

6

Consequently, the Palestinian state envisaged under the UN Partition Plan was stillborn. As is explained in the chapter on "The Palestinians and Regional Rivalries," Egypt and Syria joined the Arab side in 1948 at least as much to prevent the Hashemite monarchy of Jordan from increasing its territory and influence, as out of an altruistic desire to help the Palestinians.

The Palestinian Refugees: A Humanitarian Problem

The Palestinian Arab refugee problem emerged as a tragic consequence of the war. Whatever the reasons for their exodus, hundreds of thousands of refugees — variously estimated as between half a million and 780,000 — were living beyond Israel's frontiers set in the armistice agreements.[3] Their plight and that of their children was to be a matter of perennial concern for the United Nations in the decades that followed. In December 1949, the General Assembly established the United Nations Relief and Works Agency for Palestine Refugees in the Near East to provide emergency physical care and economic rehabilitation for the refugees. In May 1950, UNRWA launched a comprehensive program of welfare and public services, including food, clothing, shelter, medical care, education, vocational training and special hardship assistance.

The number of refugees rose constantly. For political as well as for economic reasons, families would try to conceal the death or emigration of any of its members. UNRWA contended that, for fear of riots, it was prevented from conducting an accurate census to determine the number of Palestinian Arab refugees who had died, or moved away to other countries and become economically self-sufficient. As of mid-1981, UNRWA had 1,884,896 persons on its registration rolls.

Estimates of the total number of Palestinian Arabs in 1982, both refugees and non-refugees, range from 3.6 million to 4.4 million. Of this total, there are more than one million in Jordan, 700,000 on the West Bank (Judea and Samaria), 430,000 in the Gaza District, nearly 100,000 in Jerusalem, and some 530,000 who are citizens of Israel residing within the pre-1967 Armistice lines. Thus, the great majority still live inside the boundaries of the original Palestine Mandate.

7

Approximately 350,000 Palestinians live in neighboring Lebanon and 200,000 live in Syria. Most of the others are concentrated in the Gulf region — mainly in Kuwait (270,000) and Saudi Arabia (125,000), with another 70,000 in Iraq, the United Arab Emirates, Bahrein and Qatar. In North Africa the major concentrations are in Egypt (50,000) and Libya (15,000). Estimates of the total number of Palestinians in the Americas and Europe range from 28,000 to 120,000.

Over the years (through June 1981), the United States has provided more than $933 million, or nearly half of the $2 billion spent by UNRWA. The United Kingdom, the European Economic Community, Sweden, West Germany and Japan have contributed the bulk of the rest. The Soviet Union has never given a single ruble to UNRWA, nor have the other Eastern European satellite countries, with the exception of Rumania. The Soviet Union has also refused to send any soldiers to the UN peacekeeping forces in the area. Its "contributions" to the Palestinian cause have consisted of arms and training for the Palestine Liberation Organization, and massive arms shipments to Arab states. Even while ostensibly pursuing détente with the United States, Moscow has felt free to support "movements of national liberation."

Thus, from the beginning, the Soviet Union has been concerned with the Palestinian issue as a political vehicle rather than as a humanitarian question. The Soviets also shifted their basic political support from Israel to the Arab countries once it became clear that Israel would not become a Communist satellite but a vigorously independent republic with a parliament whose majority was essentially social democratic and pro-Western in outlook. While Moscow continued to exploit Arab resentment for its own purposes, the United States pursued various initiatives designed to achieve a political solution of the Palestian question.

UN Efforts Towards a Political Solution

After armistice agreements were signed between Israel and its Arab neighbors in the spring of 1949, it was widely believed that peace would soon follow. A constructive solution to the refugee problem was anticipated within the framework of a general settlement.

On December 11, 1948, the General Assembly established the UN Conciliation Commission for Palestine (PCC) and called upon the governments concerned to "seek agreement by negotiations conducted either with the Conciliation Commission or directly, with a view to the final settlement of all questions outstanding between them." Paragraph 11 of this resolution resolved

> that the refugees wishing to return to their homes and live in peace with their neighbors should be permitted to do so at the earliest practicable date, and that compensation should be paid for the property of those choosing not to return and for loss of or damage to property which, under principles of international law or in equity, should be made good by the Governments or authorities responsible.

The Commission's task, paragraph 11 continued, was to "facilitate the repatriation, resettlement and economic and social rehabilitation of the refugees and the payment of compensation." Consisting of France, Turkey and the United States, the PCC was asked to maintain close working relations with the UN refugee agency and other appropriate UN bodies.

In April 1949, after Israel had signed armistice agreements with Egypt, Lebanon and Jordan, and begun negotiations with Syria, the Conciliation Commission met in Lausanne, Switzerland, separately with representatives of Israel and the four Arab states, to negotiate a final settlement of all outstanding questions. These indirect talks dragged on without success, for the Arabs refused to meet the Israelis face-to-face, although they had done so during the bilateral armistice negotiations.

The PCC finally adjourned the sessions and reported to the General Assembly in 1951:

> The present unwillingness of the parties fully to implement the General Assembly's resolutions...as well as the changes which have occurred in Palestine in the past three years, have made it impossible for the Commission to carry out its mandate, and this fact should be taken into consideration in any future consideration of the Palestine problem.

Why did Ralph Bunche succeed and the Conciliation Commission fail? The answer lies both in the difference of approach and the change in the objective situation. Dr. Bunche took cognizance of two important facts that subsequent negotiators ignored at their peril: 1) Underneath the façade of united anti-Israel rhetoric, the Arab states were deeply divided. Consequently, Bunche brought the Arab states and the Israelis together on a one-to-one basis. This enabled him to work out compromises based on bilateral interests. 2) Bunche realized that Egypt was the largest and most important of the Arab states, and that it was therefore necessary to begin with Cairo. The armistice agreement with Egypt was followed by similar agreements with Jordan, Lebanon and Syria — then as now the most adamant of Israel's immediate neighbors.[4]

In contrast to Dr. Bunche, a patient, skilled and persistent diplomat, the United States representative to the Conciliation Commission was a businessman lacking all familiarity with the complexities of the issues, who expected to wrap up the Arab-Israel conflict quickly. By seeking a total, comprehensive solution and treating all the Arab states as one negotiating party, the PCC assured that the outcome would be failure, since all the Arabs could agree upon was the lowest common denominator of hostility to Israel, symbolized by their delegates' refusal even to sit in the same room with the Israelis.

The objective situation, too, had changed. The armistice agreements had removed the immediate threat to the Arab states of further humiliating defeat by the Israelis. Consequently, instead of negotiating for peace, the Arabs turned to economic boycott and blockade to pursue their opposition to Israel's existence. They also turned the Palestinian Arab refugees into an instrument for this policy. The Arab states insisted that all the refugees who had lived in the territory assigned to Israel under the partition plan be returned to their homes immediately. They demanded that Israel return the territory it had won in the war the Arabs had started in 1948 because of their violent rejection of partition, and that it cede territory assigned to Israel under the partitition plan, such as the entire Negev region. Only after these demands were fulfilled, might they turn to the question of negotiating with Israel.

For their part, the Israelis were ready in Lausanne to consider the partition map as a basis for negotiation but insisted that Israel's security and the heavy losses it suffered in the war required that the armistice lines be their starting point. They also offered to permit the return of 100,000 refugees at once, but insisted that the fate of the others be determined in the course of the peace negotiations. The Arabs rejected this proposal.

From then until today, the Arab states and the PLO have acted as if paragraph 11 of the resolution of December 11, 1948, establishing the PCC, existed in a vacuum and posited the absolute right of return of all Palestinians. In fact, a close reading of the resolution as a whole and of the language of paragraph 11 itself, makes it clear that returning Palestinians must be willing to "live in peace" with their Israeli neighbors. The resolution does not speak of an absolute right of immediate return. Moreover, the Commission's mandate was to consider "resettlement" as well as repatriation. The longer the Arab-Israel dispute continued to fester, and the more Palestinian hatred of Israel grew, the more difficult it was for Israel to allow substantial numbers of refugees to return to their homes. Yet Israel did repeatedly offer to pay compensation for Arab property left behind and to assist in the resettlement of the refugees.

The Arab states strenuously resisted American and international efforts to carry out the "Works" portion of UNRWA's mandate. In January 1952, the UN General Assembly approved a $200 million budget for a three-year development fund for projects to employ and resettle Arab refugees. By the end of this period, less than 10 percent of the money had been allocated because of Arab fears that such projects would weaken the refugees' political and economic claims against Israel. Jordan was the only Arab host state to grant the refugees citizenship and to try to integrate them into its economy.

The U.S. Tries a Regional Development Approach to the Resettlement of Refugees

The Palestine Conciliation Commission had appointed Gordon Clapp of the Tennessee Valley Authority to plan large-scale development projects in the Arab countries which would also provide employment and ultimate resettlement for Palestinian refugees in Syria, northwest Sinai, and in the Yarmuk and Jordan

11

Valleys. To follow up on the Clapp mission, in the mid-1950s President Eisenhower appointed Eric Johnston as his special ambassador to negotiate a plan for the unified development of the water resources of the Jordan-Yarmuk River basin. Although Arab water engineers had reached an agreement with Israeli technicians on a fair division of the waters among Syria, Jordan and Israel, the plan was shelved at an Arab League meeting in October 1955, when Syria vetoed any development scheme that even implied recognition of — let alone cooperation with — Israel.

Subsequently Israel and Jordan developed their own national water projects in a way generally consistent with the Johnston plan and with help from the United States. But the Syrians persisted in their project, which the Arab League had backed in 1964, to divert the headwaters of the Jordan River in order to disrupt the Israeli national water carrier and thus intensify the economic strangulation of the Jewish state. This hostile action was one of the underlying factors of the Syrian-Israeli tensions that erupted in 1967 into the Six Day War.

The Hammarskjöld Proposal

Another UN initiative to resolve the refugee problem was a thoughtful series of recommendations by Dag Hammarskjöld in June 1959. In his *Proposals for the Continuation of United Nations Assistance to Palestine Refugees,* the UN Secretary-General stressed that the economic future of the refugees was closely linked to the general development of the region. He estimated that $1.7 billion would be required to reintegrate the refugees by 1970 and that an additional $12 billion in new investment would be needed to absorb the labor force in the Arab states and Israel. Hammarskjöld suggested that capital could be provided by Israel and her neighbors, by the investment of surplus funds by oil-producing Arab states in poor Arab countries and by the infusion of $1.5 billion to $2 billion from outside the region.

Citing the area's accelerating economic growth and its important underdeveloped natural resources as encouraging factors, the UN Secretary-General urged that the refugees "be regarded not as a liability, but, more justly, as an asset for the future... and a reservoir of manpower which in the desirable general economic development will assist in creation of higher standards for the whole population."

Hammarskjöld's recommendation that the refugees be "adequately trained and equipped to take advantage of the economic opportunities that emerge," led to the development of UNRWA's vocational training programs. His regional, non-political approach also won wide support among neutral observers and UNRWA administrators, who believed that large-scale development projects would be less vulnerable to changes in the political and psychological climate if they proceeded independently of UNRWA and without reference to refugee resettlement.

The Secretary-General's favorable economic projections for the region were prescient although too conservative. The wealth at the disposal of the Arab oil producers soon far exceeded his predictions. Middle East economic development, especially in the Gulf region, attracted hundreds of thousands of Palestinians, as well as Egyptians, Jordanians, Syrians and other Arabs. Yet while many individual Palestinians benefited from this prosperity, it did not bring about the political solution that the United States and the UN Secretary-General had hoped for.

Johnson's Attempt to Find a Compromise Solution

In August 1961, at the initiative of the United States, the PCC undertook a fresh effort to solve the refugee problem in the absence of full-scale peace. Dr. Joseph Johnson, president of the Carnegie Endowment for International Peace, was appointed to explore practical approaches to the refugee question. During the next year-and-a-half, he met repeatedly with representatives of the Israeli and Arab governments, seeking their acceptance of proposals for gradual repatriation of some refugees to Israel and, simultaneously, the resettlement of the remainder in the Arab countries.

Dr. Johnson's proposals sought to establish a middle ground between the Arabs' insistence that all refugees be allowed "to return to their homes" and Israel's contention that this solution was no longer practicable because these homes had either been destroyed in the war or were now occupied by Jews — many of

13

whom were themselves refugees from Arab lands. Moreover, Israel argued, the Arab refugees had been indoctrinated with hatred against Israel for so long that their return would constitute a threat to the nation's security.

Johnson recommended the creation of a mechanism which would permit individual refugees to express their preferences freely, "insulated from heavy political pressures by those who claim to be their leaders and by politicians of the host countries." He estimated that under such circumstances, fewer than one-tenth of the "true refugees and their descendants" would wish to return to Israel.

Stressing the need to recognize that "Israel would continue to exist as a state, with a predominantly Jewish population," Johnson reiterated the UN's responsibility "not to countenance any plan that would threaten the existence of Israel or of any other Member State." He agreed that Israel could refuse to admit individuals it considered security risks, but rejected Israel's demand to limit the number of refugees it would accept.

Mindful of the Arabs' refusal to negotiate with Israel, Johnson still envisaged a "kind of tacit acquiescence" to his proposal and the parties' informal cooperation with its UN-administered implementation. But despite his initial optimism, the proposals proved unacceptable to both sides, and the effort to end the long stalemate was dropped.[5]

The Refugee Problem Turns Into a National Movement

The situation of the Palestinian Arab refugees thus became unique in the annals of post-World War II refugee migration. More than 40 million persons were made homeless after 1945 but, as Dr. Lawrence Michelmore, the Commissioner-General of UNRWA, pointed out in his report for the year ending June 30, 1965, most of them "uprooted themselves and broke with their past to seek a new life in new surroundings and in a new country." However, the Palestinian refugees "use every opportunity to stress the intensity of their aspirations and hopes to return to their former homeland." Michelmore added that the creation of the Palestine Liberation Organization had intensified the Palestinians' nationalist aspirations, complicating UNRWA's work and making the restoration of peace and stability to the Middle East more difficult.

The Six Day War profoundly altered the nature of the Palestinian question. On the one hand, Israel's occupation of the West Bank and the Gaza Strip brought more than a million additional Palestinian Arabs under Israel's *de facto* jurisdiction. Israeli Arabs suddenly made contact with relatives and neighbors from whom they had been cut off for 19 years. Israel's Open Bridges policies also made it possible for these contacts to extend to Palestinians who had moved to Jordan and to the Arab world outside.

The fears generated by the war prompted some 245,000 Arabs to leave the West Bank and Gaza for Jordan, including about 110,000 refugees of 1948 who lived in camps around Jericho. Some 80,000 to 100,000 fled from the Golan Heights to Syria. On June 14, 1967, the UN Security Council called on Israel to "facilitate the return of those inhabitants who have fled the areas since the outbreak of hostilities." Some 27,000 persons returned to the West Bank by the end of 1967, and Israel later permitted several thousand others to return under hardship and family reunion provisions.

At the UN, the United States successfully beat back efforts to censure Israel. President Lyndon Johnson announced a five-point peace program on June 19, which called for a negotiated settlement through which the Arab states formally recognized Israel's "fundamental right to live." The second point stipulated the need for "justice for the refugees." The American President noted that past mediation efforts had failed "to restore the victims of conflict to their homes or to find them other proper places to live and work." He pledged that "in a climate of peace," the nations of the Middle East could count on the United States to "do our full share" to solve the refugee problem and support regional cooperation and economic development, including nuclear-powered desalination projects to "make the deserts bloom."

UN Security Council Resolution 242, adopted unanimously on November 22, 1967, incorporated most of the major principles of President Johnson's approach and linked the call for Israeli withdrawal from occupied territory to the establishment of a just and lasting peace. The Security Council also placed the refugee problem within this broader context, affirming the necessity "for achieving a just settlement of the refugee problem..."

American representatives have confirmed that the text did not refer specifically to the *Palestinian* or to the *Arab* refugee problem because the United States believed that the claims of the Jewish refugees from Arab countries — whose numbers roughly equalled those of the Palestinian refugees — would also have to be taken into consideration in any final settlement of the Arab-Israeli conflict. Lord Caradon, Britain's delegate to the UN and the author of the compromise text that became Resolution 242, has stated that the reason that there was no reference in the resolution to a Palestinian entity or state was that none of the Arab representatives in 1967 had made any such request. The general consensus at that time was that any territory from which Israel withdrew would be restored to Egypt, Jordan and Syria, respectively.

The Six Day War greatly increased Palestinian disillusionment with the ability of the Arab states to bring about a restoration of Palestinian rights.

The General Assembly as a Vehicle for Militant PLO Demands

The PLO has been gaining increased recognition of its militant demand for Palestinian rights in the international community. At the United Nations General Assembly, the Soviet, Arab, Muslim and non-aligned groups of countries have provided a sympathetic audience and an automatic majority for the Palestinians as a Third World liberation movement.

This campaign started in December 1969, with a resolution introduced into the annual UNRWA debate in a General Assembly committee by Somalia and 11 other pro-Arab states. This committee asserted that the problem of the Palestinian Arab refugees resulted from the "denial of their inalienable rights," reaffirmed "the inalienable rights of the people of Palestine" and asked the Security Council to take effective action to implement the relevant UN resolutions. The U.S. representative pointed out that the Palestinian refugees did not have an unconditionally free choice in the matter, but that they had to agree to live at peace with their neighbors. The UN had a clear responsibility "not to countenance any proposals which threatened the existence of Israel or of any other Member State," he added.

16

The substance of the resolution was approved by a vote of 48 to 22, with 47 abstentions. Virtually all the votes in favor came from Arab, Islamic or Communist states. The vote represented a political victory of considerable propaganda value for the Palestinian "liberation" movement. It also indicated a growing tendency to regard the Palestinian problem not primarily as a humanitarian one affecting individual Arab refugees, but as a political question relating to a nationalist movement.

Over the years, the Arabs skillfully built on this resolution in order to strengthen its terms. The process reached its culmination on November 22, 1974, when the General Assembly adopted two resolutions which greatly enhanced the PLO's international position. The first (Resolution 3236) recognized that "the Palestinian people is entitled to self-determination" in accordance with the UN Charter, reaffirmed the "inalienable rights of the Palestinian people in Palestine," including self-determination, "national independence and sovereignty," and their right "to return to their homes and property from which they have been displaced and uprooted," and called for their return. While the resolution "recognizes that the Palestinian people is a principal party in the establishment of a just and durable peace in the Middle East," it also implicitly endorsed the PLO's armed struggle for liberation by stating that it "further recognizes the right of the Palestinian people to regain its rights *by all means* in accordance with the purposes and principles of the Charter of the United Nations" (emphasis added). Nowhere did the resolution refer to Israel by name or acknowledge its rights.

The resolution was adopted by a vote of 89 in favor; 8 countries voted against (Bolivia, Chile, Costa Rica, Iceland, Israel, Nicaragua, Norway, the United States), and 37 abstained.

The second resolution (3237) invited the PLO to participate as an observer in the sessions and work of the UN General Assembly, as well as in international conferences convened under the Assembly's auspices, and declared the PLO entitled to participate in conferences convened by other UN organs. This accorded the PLO a status similar to that of some non-member states, such as Switzerland and North and South Korea. The resolution was adopted by a vote of 95 to 17, with 19 abstentions. Opposed were

Israel, the United States, Canada, and some Western European and Latin American states.

Reasons for International Support of the Palestinians

The Palestinians have managed to achieve far greater international recognition, sympathy and support than other well-defined national movements, such as the Kurds, the Armenians, the Azerbaijanis, the Croatians or the Basques. There would seem to be several reasons for this: First of all, they are a highly articulate and literate group, especially those who reside abroad. (According to Palestinian sources, there are proportionately more university graduates among them than among any other Arab group.) Secondly, the focus of their struggle is Israel, a democracy with a free press and an open society. Despite restrictions of military censorship, the Palestinian issue is freely debated in Israel, and the Palestinians have access to Israeli courts to appeal their rights. Palestinian Arabs who are Israeli citizens and members of the Hadash (Communist) and left-wing Mapam parties have a platform within the Knesset even for Palestinian national aspirations opposed by the Government. Such expression is impossible for dissidents in totalitarian or authoritarian regimes. Because Israel is a democratic country, the world news media are readily able to cover events there and in the administered territories.

Thirdly, the area in dispute is the Holy Land, which evokes a natural and intense interest among Jews, Christians and Muslims around the world. A fourth reason is that Jews are prominent within the intellectual communities of most Western countries and in the forefront of liberal causes. Thus, there is considerable sympathy for the Palestinians, especially for the plight of the refugees, even on the part of Jews who reject the terrorist policies and anti-Israel stand of the PLO. Another reason is that the terrorist activities of certain Palestinian groups have drawn international attention to their grievances even when their methods have caused revulsion. Moreover, the perception that the Palestinians can damage important interests and that they are prepared to undertake extreme actions has had an intimidating effect in some quarters. And another factor, one which is hard to measure, is the extent to which the Palestinians draw support from elements who oppose a sovereign Jewish state either on theological grounds or because they are basically anti-Semitic.

Probably the most significant advantage of the Palestinians over other liberation movements is the fact that they can always count on 21 Arab UN members to support them. They can also be sure of the support of the 42-member Islamic bloc and, since 1951, of the more or less automatic backing of the Soviet Union and the other countries of the Socialist bloc. By defining the Zionist enemy as "racist" and an agent of imperialism, the Palestinians have managed to strike a responsive chord among many of the newly independent states of the Third World. Yet a considerable number of these states, notably the ones in Africa, have had practical experience with Israeli technical cooperation and training missions, and they know from personal experience that these characterizations of Israel are false. In their case there is a more pragmatic reason for voting in favor of extreme pro-Palestinian resolutions at the United Nations and other international forums: Supporting pro-Palestinian resolutions is a quid pro quo for support by the large Arab and Islamic bloc of the Africans' concerns regarding South Africa, Namibia and Zimbabwe.

The same principle has operated with respect to Greece and Turkey, whose governments have vied with one another in expressing support for the Palestinians and in establishing PLO offices in their capitals: Both Athens and Ankara seek to obtain Arab voting support at the UN for their respective positions on the Cyprus dispute.

Finally, most Third World countries — even more than the Europeans — have in recent years become increasingly dependent on oil and economic concessions from the Arab oil producers. Supporting the PLO at the UN is a relatively inexpensive way of scoring points among their Arab creditors.

Attitude of the Western European Nations

Although the Western European states have generally abstained rather than openly supported the extreme pro-PLO rhetoric at the United Nations, they too have moved closer to advocacy of Palestinian self-determination, more so than the United States.

While demanding Arab recognition of Israel's sovereignty and security, the West Europeans, through their 1980 Venice Declaration, also support Palestinian self-determination, including "association" of the PLO in the Arab-Israel peace process. These nations contend that they are motivated solely by considerations of equity and fairness, claiming that the long involvement of some of them, notably Britain and France, in the affairs of the Middle East gives them special knowledge and a special responsibility. The more cynical explanation is that the Europeans are also interested in securing Arab oil and in obtaining Middle East markets for their armaments, for their construction companies, and for their industrial and consumer products.

The most dramatic shift has occurred in the case of France; in fact, it preceded the Six Day War. In May 1967, after Egyptian President Gamal Abdel Nasser removed the United Nations Emergency Force and proclaimed the reimposition of the blockade against Israeli shipping through the Straits of Tiran, Israel embarked on a major diplomatic campaign to enlist the support of the United States and the Western maritime powers who, in 1957, had affirmed its right to free passage through the straits as part of the conditions for Israeli withdrawal from Sinai and the establishment of UNEF.

The reaction of France's President Charles de Gaulle was to warn Israel "not to fire the first shot," and to impose an embargo on arms shipments to Israel. When Israeli Foreign Minister Abba Eban reminded de Gaulle that France had been among the most ardent champions in 1957 of Israel's right to take military action if necessary to assert its maritime rights, interference with which constituted a *casus belli*, de Gaulle reportedly responded, "But that was in 1957, we are now in 1967."

What had changed was not international law. On the contrary, the International Law of the Sea conference of 1958 had explicitly recognized the right of passage through straits such as that necessary for Israel's access to its port of Eilat. What de Gaulle meant was that France's relations with the Arab world had undergone a fundamental change. In the mid-1950s France had worked closely with Israel and supplied it with arms because both countries saw Nasser as a major threat to their interests. France was

20

concerned primarily with Nasser's support of the FLN against the French in Algeria. But after France granted independence to Algeria in 1962, the French were interested in maintaining economic and cultural ties with the newly independent countries of the Maghreb — Morocco, Tunisia and Algeria — and with improving relations with the rest of the Arab world, particularly with the oil producers. Thus, even before the outbreak of the Six Day War, France was moving toward neutrality in the Arab-Israel conflict. Israel's preemptive strike provided de Gaulle with the excuse to give that neutrality a decidedly pro-Arab tilt.

De Gaulle's successors followed the same policy. The new Socialist government of François Mitterand has promised a more balanced policy, one that is more friendly to Israel and sensitive to its security concerns, while continuing to affirm Palestinian rights. It is too early to tell to what extent this will be translated into deeds, e.g., arms sales to Israel and a restriction of nuclear fuel supplies to Iraq. The anticipated continuation of the current oil glut may also lessen the leverage of the Arab OPEC members on Western Europe.

Increasing Soviet Support for the PLO

While the Soviet Union has generally adopted a pro-Arab stance in the Arab-Israel conflict since the early 1950s, the degree of its support for the PLO was affected by its relations with individual Arab countries and also by Moscow's assessment of how it could best advance its own interests in the region — whether by ostensibly cooperating with Washington directly or under the UN umbrella, or by outright competition with the United States. After being forced by American nuclear pressure to withdraw from Iran in 1946 and to give up its demands upon Turkey and Greece as a result of the Truman Doctrine and the creation of NATO, the Soviet Union was rather quiescent in the Middle East for several years. In the early 1950s, the main Communist challenge to the West was posed far from the Middle East, in the war over Korea.

Ironically, it was not the unsettled Palestinian question but U.S. Secretary of State John Foster Dulles's effort to close the ring of containment around the Soviet Union that provided Moscow with a new opportunity to extend its influence in the region. Seeing a gap between NATO and SEATO, Dulles attempted to create a

"Northern Tier" defense alliance linking Turkey, Iran and Pakistan. Baghdad became the headquarters of the new alliance in 1955, enabling the British to transform their increasingly hated bilateral treaty with Iraq into a broader regional defense pact. The U.S. and Britain then made efforts to bring Jordan and other Arab states into the Baghdad Pact.

But for the Arabs, the struggle against British imperialism, their concern over their place in the interregional balance of power, as well as their continuing resentment against Israel, had a far higher priority than the fear of Communist expansion in the Middle East. As Western arms — ostensibly to be used only in defense against Soviet aggression or subversion — poured into Pakistan, India's ire was aroused. President Nasser of Egypt, who sought to become the leader of the Arab, Islamic and African contingents, was even more angered by the Baghdad Pact — his historic and natural rivals for leadership in the region, Turkey and Iraq, were to be militarily and politically strengthened. Damascus, which fancied itself the leader of a Greater Syria that encompassed the Fertile Crescent, was similarly upset.

Skillfully exploiting these resentments, Moscow concluded massive arms deals and initiated close cooperation with Egypt and Syria, in effect leapfrogging the paper barrier that Dulles had erected with the Middle East Treaty Organization, as the Baghdad Pact was formally known. Riots inspired by Communists and Nasserists in Jordan kept that country in turmoil, and the revolution that overthrew the monarchy in Iraq in July 1958 ended Baghdad's own participation in the pact. Lebanon was wracked by civil war; after its government invited U.S. Marines to intervene, the contending factions were brought to an uneasy truce that lasted a decade. The U.S. had stepped in under the terms of the Eisenhower Doctrine, offering help to any Middle East country threatened by international communism.

The numerous pitfalls that led to the dismal failure of the American effort to forge an anti-Soviet alliance in the Middle East in the Eisenhower-Dulles era should well be kept in mind by the policy makers of the Reagan Administration as they seek to develop a "strategic consensus" in the Middle East. While much has changed since the 1950s, the rivalries within the region have by no means diminished. As for the Soviet Union, it has displayed a greater capacity and readiness to intervene than before. While the Soviets suffered reverses — notably the expulsion of its advisors from Egypt and the exclusion of Moscow from the Camp David process that has led to the Egyptian-Israeli peace treaty — the West's position, too, was weakened, by Britain's withdrawal from Aden and the Persian Gulf in 1969 and, more recently, by the overthrow of the pro-Western Shah in Iran.

Moscow's arming and rearming of the Arab confrontation states has been accompanied by more formalized ties with Libya, the Marxist Peoples Republic of (South) Yemen, Iraq and Syria. At the same time it has also upgraded its relationship with the PLO. The USSR first placed the Palestinian struggle in the category of "national liberation movements" in 1969 — the year the PLO won its first major victory at the United Nations. Moscow called for recognition of the Palestinians' "legitimate national rights" after the Yom Kippur War in October 1973. At the time the United States was still referring only to the legitimate "interests" of the Palestinians.

After the Soviet Union formally participated in the Geneva Conference at the end of 1973, the United States, represented by Secretary of State Henry Kissinger, played the exclusive mediatory role of arranging Egyptian-Israeli disengagement agreements. Failure to work out a similar agreement on the Jordanian front — which had been quiescent during the war — left King Hussein empty-handed and may have helped his opponents crown the PLO as the sole legitimate representative of the Palestinians at the Rabat summit conference held in the fall of 1974. Soviet leadership was openly advocating the creation of a Palestinian state at the time, although it was still ambivalent about the PLO's role. The PLO was permitted to open an office in Moscow in 1976, but it was accredited to the African-Asian Solidarity Committee, a non-governmental organization.

Yasir Arafat, the PLO leader, met with Leonid Brezhnev for the first time in April 1977. Only 19 months later, in a joint communiqué following a meeting between Arafat and Premier Aleksei Kosygin, did the Soviet Union formally refer to the PLO as the "sole" legitimate representative of the Palestinians.

Still, it was only on October 28, 1981, that Brezhnev informed Arafat, at the conclusion of their meeting in Moscow, that the Soviet Union had decided to extend full diplomatic status to the PLO. The Soviets had been considering such a move even before Anwar Sadat's death, and Western political observers believe that Moscow's decision "should be seen as part of the USSR's broad effort in 1981 to reassert its role as a player in the Middle East peace process."[6] The Soviet effort was launched at the 26th Communist Party Congress in February 1981. In May, the PLO initially approved Brezhnev's proposal for a new international conference to replace Camp David, as did Jordan's King Hussein during his visit to Moscow.

It would be ironic if the recent successes Arafat has scored in Western European capitals and in Japan finally convinced the Soviet Union that it could not appear to be a less firm supporter of the PLO than the capitalist states. Brezhnev reportedly told Arafat:

> The Palestinian people have accomplished substantial successes in [their] struggle and moved to the forefront of the Arab national liberation movement, while their political vanguard, the Palestine Liberation Organization, has secured extensive international recognition as the sole legitimate representative of the Palestinian people.[7]

There are some who believe that Moscow may exert a moderating influence on the PLO, but the failure of the PLO to support the Fahd plan, which does not even explicitly mention recognition of Israel, should make one skeptical. In view of continued Soviet military support of the rejectionist states of Libya, Iraq, Syria and South Yemen, Moscow's expressed concern for Israel's security is viewed with natural suspicion in Jerusalem. The meeting between the Soviet Union's Andrei Gromyko and Israel's Yitzhak Shamir at the UN in New York in September 1981 — the first meeting between the foreign ministers of the two countries in six years — did not lead to a resumption of the relations that Moscow had broken off in 1967. While Gromyko urged Israel to support Brezhnev's idea of an international conference, Shamir stressed Israel's grave concern at the sharp decline in Soviet-Jewish emigration.

24

Prime Minister Begin of Israel, President Hosni Mubarak of Egypt and President Reagan have all recently reaffirmed their commitment to the continuation of the Camp David peace process. But if no progress is made on the Palestinian autonomy discussions, there will certainly be renewed international pressures to adopt another approach. Before Americans become beguiled by the seemingly simple solution of an international conference to solve the Palestinian question and achieve a comprehensive peace, they would do well to recall the dismal failure of similar efforts and ask themselves whether Moscow's actions in the Middle East in the past, and its policies at present — in Afghanistan, in Poland, its formal support of the PLO — make it a suitable partner to achieve the genuine and lasting peace in the Middle East that it is in accord with American vital interests.

Notes

1. The Palestine Liberation Organization Covenant's denial of Jewish nationalism and of the historical connection of Jews to Palestine thus runs counter to the unanimous judgment of the League Council. The PLO Covenant specifically denounces both the Balfour Declaration and the Mandate.

2. The name Cis-Jordan ("on this side of the Jordan") never caught on as a parallel to Transjordan. To add to the semantic confusion, after Transjordan's annexation of some territory in Palestine west of the Jordan River following the Arab-Israeli war of 1948, the Hashemite Kingdom changed its name from Transjordan to Jordan. Since that time, the term "West Bank" has been limited to this western portion of the Jordanian Kingdom, to distinguish it from the territory that became the State of Israel, or from the Gaza Strip, even though geographically speaking, all three lie on the West Bank of the Jordan River.

3. Professor Edward Said concludes that according to "the most precise calculation yet made, approximately 780,000 Arab Palestinians were dispossessed and displaced in 1948" (*The Question of Palestine* [New York: Vintage Division of Random House, 1980], p. 14). Dr. Walter Pinner estimates that the number of refugees in May 1948 did not exceed 539,000. See *How Many Refugees?* (London: Macgibbon & Kee, 1959). A detailed demographic and political comparison between the experience of the Jewish refugees from Arab countries and that of the Palestinian Arab refugees is provided by Dr. Maurice M. Roumani in *The Case of the Jews from Arab Countries*, Second edition (Tel Aviv: WOJAC, 1978).

4. Iraq refused to sign an armistice agreement, thus maintaining the purity of its ideological opposition to Israel. It contended that no agreement was necessary since Iraq had no contiguous border with Israel. Moreover, since the rulers at that time of Jordan and Iraq were Hashemite cousins, Baghdad was ready to let Amman act in its behalf.

5. The quotations are from *Arab vs. Israeli: A Persistent Challenge to Americans,* Address by Dr. Johnson to the American Assembly of Columbia University, Oct. 24, 1963. For additional details, see George E. Gruen, *The Arab Refugee Problem and the United Nations*, Reports on the Foreign Scene (New York: AJC, April 1966), No. 7, pp. 7-8.

6. Robert Rand, "The USSR Extends Full Diplomatic Recognition to the PLO," *Radio Liberty Research*, Oct. 21, 1981.

7. Tass News Agency, Oct. 20, 1981.

George E. Gruen

THE PALESTINIANS AND REGIONAL RIVALRIES

There has always been tension between the Arabs' ideological yearning for pan-Arab unity and the centrifugal pressures exerted by the distinct and often conflicting interests of individual Arab states. The Palestinian issue has been a focus of this tension, and the Palestinian people both its tool and its victim.

The poles of union and separatism were graphically illustrated in February 1977, when an American interreligious study mission to the Middle East visited the elegant headquarters of the Arab League, then in Cairo. We were first shown a large map of "the Arab World" showing, circled in red, the vast area stretching from Morocco on the Atlantic to Iraq and Saudi Arabia on the Persian Gulf. There were no internal borders between countries and there was, of course, no indication of Israel's existence. We were then ushered in to the Arab League Council chamber, where special markers on the green felt-covered table and the ornate gilded chairs around it were inscribed with the names of the 22 member states of the Arab League, including one of the Palestine Liberation Organization as representative of "Palestine." Each Arab state zealously guards its sovereignty and all major League decisions require unanimity to be binding. (After Egypt concluded a peace treaty with Israel, the Arab League moved its headquarters "temporarily" to Tunisia.)

We asked the League official who was guiding us, "How do you explain the contradiction between the borderless map in the next room and the plethora of sovereign Arab states represented in the Council chamber?" "The Council," he answered, "reflects the Arab reality of today, the map represents our ideal for the future."

A Dilemma: A Palestinian State vs. Arab Unity

The Palestinian question has had a paradoxical impact on inter-Arab relations. On the one hand, it has served as an emotional rallying point. The defeat and dispersion of the Palestinians in 1948 was seen as a defeat for the Arabs in general, and thus a national humiliation. The struggle to erase that defeat, plus hatred for Israel, provided a common external enemy against which the Arabs could unite. Indeed, once the anti-colonial battle had been won and the Arab states had achieved independence, the anti-Israel campaign was probably the only cause that could unify the deeply divided Arab world and provide a practical focus for the long-sought but always elusive goal of Arab unity.

On the other hand, when the Palestine Liberation Organization was founded in 1964, its objective was to create yet another distinctive Arab state; and it faced the dilemma of reconciling this aim with the larger goal of Arab unity. In an attempt to deal with this apparent contradiction, Article 1 of the PLO Covenant proclaimed that "Palestine is an Arab homeland bound by strong Arab national ties to the rest of the Arab countries, which together form the great Arab homeland." And there is a suggestion of apology in Article 12, which states that "The Palestinian people believe in Arab unity. In order to contribute their share toward the attainment of that objective, however, they must, at the present stage of their struggle, safeguard their Palestinian identity and develop their consciousness of that identity, and oppose any plan that may dissolve or impair it."

The geographic extent of the Palestinian homeland quickly became a bone of contention with Jordan. When the Covenant was drafted, Ahmad Shuqayri, the first leader of the PLO, assured King Hussein that the organization intended to liberate only the area west of the Hashemite Kingdom of Jordan, that is, the State of Israel. But friction soon developed over PLO activities within the country and on the West Bank, which was then under Jordanian control. Article 2 of the PLO Covenant stipulates that "Palestine, with the boundaries it had during the British Mandate, is an indivisible territorial unit." But since Jordan had, in February 1954, extended citizenship to all Palestinians — both those who remained on the West Bank and those who had moved to the East Bank — the PLO's assertion of a distinct Palestinian identity threatened to undermine the Hashemite Kingdom's efforts to create a unified Jordanian state including Transjordan (which had become formally independent in 1946) and the West Bank territory annexed after the 1948 Arab-Israel war.

Arab Frictions After the Six Day War

After the Six Day War in 1967, friction between Jordan and the PLO intensified, as the PLO acted increasingly as a state within a state. The climax came in September 1970, when one of the most radical member groups, the Popular Front for the Liberation of Palestine, hijacked three international airliners to Jordan, blew them up at a desert airfield outside Amman, and held the passengers hostage. The Palestinian guerrillas were helped by Syria, which sent in Soviet-supplied tanks in an effort to overthrow Hussein's rule and replace it with a radical Palestinian regime. The mobilization of Israeli army and air forces, in a move coordinated with Washington and Amman, convinced the Syrian air force commander, Col. Hafez al-Assad, not to commit his planes. This move enabled Hussein to rout the Palestinian *fedayeen* groups and forced the Syrians to beat a hasty retreat. Since their rout in that "Black September," the *fedayeen* have not been permitted to operate on Jordanian territory. Within Syria itself, Assad took advantage of the debacle to stage a bloodless coup and supplant the regime of his predecessors.

The PLO regrouped and transferred its main base of operations to Lebanon, where some 350,000 Palestinian refugees live today, and where it has played a major role in further destabilizing that strife-torn country. The PLO has remained heavily dependent on Syrian support, but the relationship has been increasingly uneasy and riddled with mutual suspicion. When Palestinians allied to the Muslim leftists appeared to be winning the Lebanese civil war in 1976, Syria threw its weight behind the Christian rightists to redress the balance. The Syrian army's shelling of PLO positions in the Tel Za'atar refugee camp produced a massacre of Palestinians no less brutal than that inflicted by the Jordanian army in Black September six year earlier. Put to the test, the traditional Syrian national interest in establishing hegemony over neighboring

28

Lebanon won out over its professed commitment to the Palestinian cause. The Syrian occupation army of some 25,000 men in Lebanon was quasi-legitimized by the Arab League as the "Arab Deterrent Force." It even had the tacit approval of the United States which, at the time, saw it as a lesser evil than the prospect of total chaos or a militant Marxist takeover. The Saudis, too, discreetly financed the Syrian effort.

The naive revolutionary expectations of the Palestinian movement in the post-1967 era, and the disillusionment that followed when the existing Arab regimes successfully asserted their authority, are poignantly described by Professor Fouad Ajami, Director of Middle East Studies at the School of Advanced International Studies of Johns Hopkins University. In "The Revolution That Failed: Arab Radicals After Nasser,"[1] Ajami states that "where it had once been believed that the Arab states would liberate Palestine, it was now [after 1967] expected that the Palestinian struggle would topple the Arab order." However, through the victory of Hussein's army over the PLO in Jordan, and of Assad's forces over the PLO in Lebanon, Ajami states, "the dominant order would demonstrate not only the superiority of its firepower but also the weakness of theory disconnected from the hard facts of political life." The PLO's ideological theorists had assumed that Hussein's army — which included Palestinians but had Bedouin officers — would refuse to fight the Palestinians. But for Jordan's simple soldiers, "the fight was between the King — their chieftain, their financial provider, a man who claims descent from the Prophet — and atheistic troublemakers, townsmen with alien and offensive ways," Ajami says.

In Lebanon as well, nothing has come of the revolutionary hope expressed in 1976 by George Habash, leader of the Popular Front for the Liberation of Palestine, that the collapsed "reactionary, bourgeois confessional regime" would be replaced by a radically new "democratic, nationalist, secular Lebanon." In reality, power is still fragmented and divided among the sons of the old established families, clans, and religious and ethnic groups prominent in Lebanon before the civil war.

Ajami concludes that "to the extent that the Palestinian movement represented and embodied the post-1967 Arab revolution, its troubles burst the revolutionary bubble of the post-1967 years. There would be no easy way out; the panacea of a people's war of national liberation was but a brief illusion.... By the time the Arab armies went into action on October 6, 1973, and the reactionary oil states deployed the oil weapon, the old world had made a stand of its own; it promised its own dawn of a new age.''

The Palestine Issue as a Weapon
in Inter-Arab Rivalries

Egypt and Syria entered the October 1973 war on their own, with no significant help from the PLO, and then Egypt proceeded to make peace with Israel despite the vehement objections of the PLO. On the other hand, President Assad reaffirmed in December 1981 that ''even if the Palestine Liberation Organization recognizes Israel, we in Syria cannot recognize it.''[2] This was one more demonstration that when goals appeared to clash, the Arab states gave a higher priority to their own perceived national interests than to the demands of the Palestinians.

While the Arab states have treated the Palestinians in a cavalier fashion, it is also true that the Palestinian issue has frequently been used by one Arab state to attack another. Allegations of weakness and incompetence on this question could similarly be used in the internal politics of Arab states. For example, the defeat of the Egyptian army in the 1948 war played an important role in galvanizing its Free Officers finally to overthrow the corrupt monarchy of King Farouk.

The unsuccessful intervention by Egypt and Syria into the Palestine conflict in May 1948 was motivated at least as much by a desire to forestall an increase in the power of the Hashemites, who then ruled in both Transjordan and Iraq, as to save the Palestinian Arabs by crushing the new State of Israel. King Abdullah of Transjordan had initially agreed, in secret talks with the Zionist leadership, not to attack the UN-proposed Jewish state if the projected Palestinian state could be peacefully linked to Transjordan. But this deal came unstuck when the British failed to maintain order and the fighting between local Arabs and Jews began to escalate. When Transjordan annexed what was left of the West Bank after the 1948 war, ostensibly at the urging of a council of local notables, most of the anti-Hashemite states in the Arab League — led by Egypt, Syria and Saudi Arabia — pushed for

Jordan's expulsion. A compromise could be struck only when Jordan pledged it was holding the territory "in trust" for the Palestinians only until a final settlement of the entire problem could be reached.

Because King Abdullah had begun to negotiate peace with Israel after the 1948 war, he was assassinated in 1951 on his way to prayers at the al-Aqsa Mosque in Jerusalem by a Palestinian supporter of the Mufti, Hajj Amin al-Husseini. (Similarly, in the 1930s, the Mufti's supporters in the Arab Higher Committee for Palestine had systematically killed several hundred Palestinian Arab moderates suspected of readiness to negotiate a compromise with the Zionists.)

Attacking enemies in the Arab world as tools or agents of Zionism, or otherwise undermining them, has become so frequent a tactic that it has been named "outbidding"; and even the PLO has been "outbid." For example, on October 15, 1965, a year after it had been founded, Arab states requested that a PLO delegation to the UN "representing the Arab people of Palestine, the principal party to the Palestine question," be heard during the annual debate on the functioning and financing of the United Nations Relief and Works Agency for Palestine Refugees in the Near East (UNRWA). And the UN's special political committee did permit persons in the PLO delegation to speak — but "without such authorization implying recognition of their group." (Another decade was to pass before the PLO reached its present uniquely favored position as observer, which enables it to enjoy virtually all the prerogatives of a UN member state except the right to vote.)

With the same limitation, the UN committee in 1965 also granted a hearing to a spokesman of the "Palestine Arab Delegation" sponsored by the Arab Higher Committee for Palestine. The Mufti's group, which had moved its headquarters to Syria, denounced the PLO as a tool of "Zionist and imperialist elements." To underscore the ineffectiveness of the Egyptian-supported PLO, which until then had taken no serious action against Israel, Syria and the Mufti reportedly backed the rival Fatah guerrilla group, which had made its first terrorist attack on Israel in January 1965.

During 1965, despite growing opposition in Jordan and Lebanon, the PLO continued its efforts to recruit a "Palestine Liberation Army" from refugees in the Gaza Strip. Although the Liberation

31

Army is officially the military arm of the PLO, the fact is that its units have been controlled by the respective Arab countries to whose conventional armed forces they are attached. These army units have even, at times, fought against some of the PLO's *fedayeen* (guerrilla) groups, as was the case in Lebanon.

In general, scholars believe that the inter-Arab process of "outbidding" on the Palestinian issue was a precipitating factor in the Six Day War. The Soviet Union had tried to sponsor a rapprochement between the embittered Egyptians and Syrians after their United Arab Republic (1958-1961) fell apart. Both Egypt and Syria were Soviet-supported states embroiled in a campaign to overthrow the pro-Western monarchy in Jordan, and Cairo radio regularly referred to King Hussein as the "Hashemite whore" paid by Zionism and imperialism. In turn, the Jordanians goaded Egyptian President Gamal Abdel Nasser to prove he was indeed a militant leader of the Palestinian struggle, accusing him of "hiding behind the skirts" of the United Nations Emergency Force (UNEF) which had been insulating him since the 1956 Sinai Campaign from taking military action against Israel. Challenged by the escalation of air clashes between Syria and Israel, Nasser decided to demonstrate his leadership by mobilizing forces in the Sinai, telling the UNEF to step aside, and renewing the blockade against Israeli shipping. Caught up in the frenzied anti-Israel rhetoric, Hussein went to Cairo and joined the Egyptian-Syrian alliance. When, to break out of its hostile encirclement, Israel launched its preemptive strike against Egypt and Syria on June 5, 1967, it urgently appealed to Hussein to stay out of the conflict. He refused.

After Egypt's, Syria's and Jordan's defeat in the Six Day War, Shuqayri was ousted from the PLO leadership and replaced in February 1969 by Yasir Arafat, who had been heading the rival Syrian-backed Fatah group.

The Palestinian issue is still a weapon in inter-Arab rivalries. When Arab rejectionists accused President Sadat of having sold out the Palestinians at Camp David by signing a peace treaty with Israel, he countercharged that the Egyptian people had borne the brunt of fighting and sacrifice in four wars to safeguard Palestinian rights, while the Gulf states "grew rich on oil." Every major Arab state has created or supported a faction in the Palestinian movement and has tried to influence the decisions of the PLO and the Palestinian National Council, the unofficial parliamentary assembly. Thus the PLO reflects all the diverse elements and conflicting tendencies in the Arab world, with the possible exception of those among the half-million Palestinian Arabs who are citizens of Israel.

To maintain the PLO leadership, Arafat has had constantly to shift and adjust tactics in order to steer a course between those conflicting elements, which has severely limited his freedom of action and given veto power to hard-line extremists. He is more the chairman of a loose conglomerate, each of whose divisions feels free to act on its own, than a strong chief executive who can impose his will. Because the PLO is weakened by open conflicts among its supporters, he has tried to be a mediator, as in the case of the Iran-Iraq war, or to avoid taking a stand, as when the Soviet Union — a major military and political supporter — was condemned by Saudi Arabia and others among the PLO's Islamic backers for suppressing the Afghani people's struggle for self-determination.

The Rabat Paradox:
Theoretical Monopoly of Power and Practical Impotence

In 1974, the Arab League Summit Conference in Rabat, Morocco,proclaimed the PLO the "sole, legitimate representative of the Palestinian people"; the UN General Assembly granted it special observer status in the fall of that year; and since then it has greatly expanded its contacts and offices around the world, achieving levels of status ranging from information bureaus to quasi-official embassies. And yet, while scoring a new diplomatic success almost every month during visits to Moscow, Tokyo, Athens and so on, Arafat has been increasingly hemmed in and restricted in operations within the crucial Middle East.

Despite Jordan's nominal adherence to the Rabat Conference decision, King Hussein has refused to allow the PLO to reestablish bases in Jordan from which to attack Israel. Jordanian subsidies continue to flow to Palestinians on the West Bank, but periodic efforts to work out a rapprochement between the King and Arafat have foundered not only over the issue of primacy within a joint committee for the disbursement of funds, but — more fundamentally — over ultimate control of the Palestinians in Jordan and the West Bank.

The latest two Arab summit conferences clearly illustrated the pressures on the PLO. In November 1980, when the Syrians successfully pressed it to stay away from the summit in Amman, Jordan, analysts noted that despite the conference's "public support for the PLO as the legitimate representative of the Palestinian people, the organization was clearly warned that its future legitimacy in the eyes of the conferees depended on whether it acted independently of Syrian pressure."[3] In other words, the conference raised Hussein's inter-Arab status from its low point at Rabat, so that some pro-Western Arabs saw him as a potential spokesman to the newly elected Reagan administration on Arab and Palestinian demands.

To demonstrate its veto power over any independent Palestinian initiative by Hussein, the Syrian Government massed more than 30,000 troops along the border with Jordan; and it charged him with aiding and harboring Muslim Brotherhood terrorists who sought to overthrow Assad. Syria's official newspaper, *Tishrin,* combined those two issues in an editorial warning that "Jordan is being used as a base by Muslim extremists, and under no circumstances will Syria allow Jordan to become a base or conduit for imperialist and Zionist reactionaries."

Yet Assad did not dare actually to invade Jordan and succeeded only in deepening divisions within the Arab world: Only Algeria, Marxist Southern Yemen, Syrian-dominated Lebanon and Soviet-supported and radical Libya joined the boycott of the Amman summit. King Hussein accused Syria of "stabbing Iraq in the back" by supplying Iran in the war that had broken out in September 1980, and the Arab League summit endorsed Iraqi war aims against Iran. The conference also strengthened the emerging rapprochement among Jordan, Iraq and Saudi Arabia.

While the Amman summit again rejected the Camp David accords and reaffirmed the Palestinians' right to self-determination, Arafat and Assad feared that Saudi Arabia, Iraq and Jordan might form an axis, along with Persian Gulf oil sheikhdoms, that would emphasize the Gulf region's security and prosperity, and distract primary attention from the Arab-Israel conflict.

Damascus faced a dilemma: If the Egyptian-Israeli peace treaty was solidified and the other Arabs turned to their own national priorities, Syria would be left to face the Israelis alone. Assad knew he had virtually no hope, under these circumstances, of winning militarily or obtaining significant concessions from Israel. But if he was unwilling to negotiate, he had also to fear that if the stalemate continued, and if Israel consolidated its ground positions in the West Bank and Gaza, some Palestinians might be tempted to follow Sadat's example. They might conclude that if war in the near future was not a credible option, they had better seek a negotiated settlement before Israel's control of the occupied territories became irreversible.

Internecine Warfare in the PLO

To present a façade of unity to the outside world, the PLO has usually covered sharp divisions in the Palestinian community and among Arab states with ringing public declarations of solidarity with the Palestinian struggle at the United Nations and other international forums. Beneath the surface is a bitter fight, one of whose most bizarre examples of intrigue was revealed in September 1981 when Austria uncovered a plot to assassinate PLO chief Yasir Arafat. Implicated in the conspiracy were Ghazi Hussein, the PLO representative in Vienna and a member of the Syria-sponsored guerrilla group *as-Saiqa,* and Sabri Khalil Bannah — code-named Abu Nidal — a notorious Palestinian terrorist who had recently exchanged the protective mantle of Iraq's secret service for that of the Syrians. According to evidence in the hands of Austrian officials, Syria and Abu Nidal had deliberately attempted to leave a trail that would implicate Iraq and Jordan, Syria's rivals, in the murder.

While Syria has ostensibly been among the PLO's major supporters, "it has always been a marriage of convenience," a PLO official in Beirut confided to a *Washington Post* reporter. "We Palestinians detest the Syrians and they detest us. But we have to live together, all the same." [4] Earlier in 1981, at a closed session of the Palestinian National Council in Damascus, Arafat had said to the Syrians: "When President Assad said to me that Palestine is south Syria, I reminded him that Syria is north Palestine." [5] Some PLO officials suspected that Syria, concerned that the independent-minded, diplomatically adroit and tactically slippery Arafat might yet be tempted to accept Western European or Saudi proposals for a settlement of the Arab-Israel conflict, wanted to replace him with a puppet Palestinian who could be fully controlled by Damascus.

Middle East analysts believe that had the Abu Nidal plot succeeded, Syria would have been able to wipe out pro-Iraqi forces in Lebanon, exterminate the so-called "moderate" Fatah wing of the PLO, take effective control of the Palestinian resistance movement, and perhaps undermine the regimes of Saddam Hussein in Baghdad and King Hussein in Amman.

Abu Nidal, a former member of Arafat's own Fatah group, had been expelled from the organization and in 1974 sentenced to death in absentia for killing several Fatah and other mainline PLO representatives and Syrian officials (he was working for Baghdad at the time). He shared Iraq's radical position that the "Zionist entity" had to be extirpated by force and that the Palestinians should under no circumstances even consider a peaceful negotiated solution of the Arab-Israel conflict. After Sadat's peacemaking trip to Jerusalem, the Arab states opposed to this initiative gathered in Baghdad and tried to set aside their internal disputes. The Iraqis, in a conciliatory gesture to Arafat, agreed to rein in Abu Nidal and curtail his activities, and quietly expelled him in 1979. By the time he took up residence in Syria in 1981, the traditional animosity between the rival factions of the ruling Ba'ath (Arab Socialist Renaissance Party) in Damascus and Baghdad had been intensified by Saddam Hussein's fury at Syria's support of non-Arab Iran in its war against a fellow Arab nation. Noting the tight control of the secret police over Palestinians within Syria, pro-Arafat Palestinians and Western observers believe that Abu Nidal and his band of fanatics could not have operated openly from a base in Damascus without approval of Assad's intelligence agency.

In the meantime, in August 1981, there had been credible reports that President Sadat was the target for assassination by Palestinians on a scheduled visit to Vienna after his return from the United States, so the visit was cancelled. Austrian Interior Minister Erwin Lane declared *persona non grata* the PLO's representative, Saiqa-supporter Ghazi Hussein, for helping to smuggle arms for use by the assassins. It was during the investigation of this plot that the Abu Nidal-Syrian-Saiqa linkages first emerged. Sources close to Arafat claimed that Ghazi Hussein had leaked reports to Austrian newspapers that the PLO, not Abu Nidal, was behind the Sadat assassination attempt; one of Arafat's aides at the time, in a cynical and rather prophetic assessment, said that this assassination would fundamentally change area politics and create a serious challenge to Arafat's leadership. "Syria would love to see Israel wipe out the PLO. If only the political shell of the PLO remains, they will be able to fill it with their own men."[6]

Although Egyptian Muslim fundamentalists, not radical Palestinians, killed Sadat two months later, the innumerable divisions within the Arab world have continued, as has the challenge to Arafat's leadership. These divisions were glaringly revealed to the world at the Arab League summit conference in Fez, Morocco, abruptly called off by its host, King Hassan, when it threatened to turn into a stormy debate over the Saudi "peace plan."

Fahd Loses at Fez

When Crown Prince Fahd first revealed the Saudi plan in an interview over Riyadh radio on August 7, 1981, President Sadat — then meeting with President Reagan in Washington — dismissed it as nothing new. Many observers speculated that the Saudis' timing had been determined by a desire to impress the American Congress, which was about to consider their request for AWACS planes and other equipment to enhance the military capability of the F-15s already being sold to them. They wanted to demonstrate that notwithstanding a declared commitment to *jihad* (holy war) against Israel at the Islamic conference they had hosted at Taif (Mecca) earlier in the year, the Saudis were really prepared for a peaceful solution of the Arab-Israel conflict.

Saudi Arabia's official explanation of its "peace" initiative was that it was designed to produce an Arab consensus and to win international support for a plan that could replace the Camp David accords, "whose failure has been proven," Fahd said. He hoped the Reagan Administration would accept "the uselessness of the Camp David agreements" and initiate "a drastic change in American policy" which would demonstrate that the U.S. was "less biased toward Israel and more equitable toward the Arabs."

Fahd said that Saudi Arabia and the United States had cooperated effectively to achieve a *de facto* cease-fire in Lebanon; and turning to the Arab-Israel conflict, he proceeded to set out "principles which may be taken as guidelines toward a just settlement," emphasizing that they were not just his own views but principles approved and reiterated by the United Nations. (Fahd was referring to General Assembly resolutions which, in their support of Arab and Palestinian demands, went far beyond UN Security Council Resolutions 242 and 338, on which the Camp David accords were based.)

There are eight points in the Fahd plan:

1. Israel should withdraw from all Arab territory occupied in 1967, including Arab Jerusalem.

2. Israeli settlements built on Arab land after 1967 should be dismantled.

3. Freedom of worship for all religions in the holy places should be guaranteed.

4. The right of the Palestinian people to return to their homes, and to compensation for those who do not wish to return, should be reaffirmed.

5. There should be a transitional period, under the auspices of the United Nations and not exceeding several months, for the West Bank and the Gaza Strip.

6. An independent Palestinian state should be set up, with Jerusalem as its capital.

7. The states of the region should be able to live in peace.

8. The United Nations or its member states should guarantee to execute these principles.

Crown Prince Fahd called on the UN Security Council to consolidate these points in a new and binding resolution. He appealed to the U.S. to end its unlimited support for Israel, to bring an "end to Israeli arrogance" and to recognize that, "as Yasir Arafat says, the Palestinian figure is the basic figure in the Middle East equation." And he asked Great Britain and other countries in the European Economic Community to share the task of bringing the Arab and American positions closer together.

When Prince Saud al-Faisal, the Saudi Foreign Minister, formally presented it to the UN General Assembly on October 6,

1981, the Fahd plan — until then treated as remarks in a press interview — was elevated in status to an official statement of Saudi policy. After the assassination of Sadat on the same day, the Saudis doubled their efforts to win Arab and Palestinian support for the Fahd principles and were confident, at first, of approval by an Arab consensus at the Fez summit in November. Western and Middle East observers surmised that the Saudis, considering their successes in Lebanon, their victory in the AWACS deal, and the vacuum created by Sadat's death, believed the time opportune to play a more publicly assertive role in inter-Arab affairs.

Ever mindful of the PLO's dependence on Saudi financial aid, Arafat at first supported the Fahd plan, calling it a "good beginning" and "a good basis for a lasting peace." The Israel Government rejected the plan, seeing it as an attempt to dismantle Israel by stages, first cutting it back to indefensible borders and then flooding it with returning refugees. Some Israelis, such as Moshe Arens, then Chairman of the Foreign Affairs and Defense Committee in the Knesset and currently Israel's Ambassador in Washington, rejected the specific terms but welcomed any sign that the Saudis might be moving from advocacy of *jihad* to tacit acceptance of Israel as a state in the region. In his own rejection of the Fahd plan, Prime Minister Begin reiterated an earlier invitation to the Saudi leaders to meet anywhere without preconditions.

But when pressed on this issue, the Saudis backtracked and refused to say that Point 7 constituted recognition of Israel.[7] Arafat's deputy on the Fatah Central Committee, Salah Khalaf (Abu Iyad), specifically ruled out acceptance of that point, arguing that the PLO as a liberation organization "has no right to recognize Israel because it operates outside the occupied territory." When a Palestinian state has been established "it will enjoy sovereign rights which include its right to recognize or not." But, he added, the Palestinians were not bound by the specific terms of the Saudi proposal — for example, they would not be satisfied by Israel's withdrawal to the pre-1967 lines. "The Arabs must not propose any initiatives" he stressed, "which would conflict with the concepts, principles and the firm national right of the Palestinian people."[8] Similarly, Arafat told the Abu Dhabi daily *Al-Ittihad* that while he "had welcomed Prince Fahd's statement," he would not accept coexistence with the "Israeli enemy."[9]

Even after Arafat and Abu Iyad had specifically dissociated themselves from Point 7, they were subjected to pressure even from mainline elements in Fatah, and the PLO Executive Committee overwhelmingly decided not to endorse the Fahd plan. In their judgment, said Faruq Qaddoumi, head of the PLO's Political Department, it was tactically "inopportune, unacceptable and dangerous," for the Palestinians to accept a solution "unless the current balance of power changes in our favor."

In this approach, the PLO officials meeting in Damascus were at odds with elected Palestinian leaders in the West Bank and Gaza. Although ostensibly supporters of the PLO, the mayors of 11 cities and towns "declared support for the Saudi peace plan and urged Arab leaders to adopt" it at the Fez summit, according to the Saudi newspaper *Al-Riyad,* whose correspondent had phoned them from New York. The mayors, including those from such major Palestinian centers as Nablus, Hebron and Gaza, called on the Arab countries to work for "a rapid settlement of the Palestinian problem."[10] While PLO leaders in Beirut, Damascus and more distant places were prepared to bide their time, the Palestinians in day-to-day contact with Israel were eager to grasp any Arab proposal that offered to bring a speedy end to the Israeli occupation.

In January 1982, Mayor Elias Freij of Bethlehem went beyond endorsing the Fahd plan, with its ambiguous and indirect allusion to Israel, and publicly called on the Arab states and the PLO to recognize Israel and negotiate a formal peace. On January 24, Gaza's Mayor Rashad al-Shawwa endorsed Freij's appeal, but other West Bank mayors said Israel and the U.S. should first recognize the PLO.

While some of Arafat's Fatah colleagues had objected to the Fahd plan on tactical grounds, others in the PLO and the Arab rejectionist states had far more fundamental reasons. At the foreign ministers' session preceding the Fez summit, 'Abd al-'Ati al-'Ubaydi, Libya's Secretary for Foreign Liaison, described the plan as a "flagrant violation of the PLO Charter," declared that anyone prepared to recognize Israel should be punished by death, and asked rhetorically why the Saudi cry for *jihad* had lately become a call for "capitulation." All the radical leftist groups in the PLO — the Popular Front for the Liberation of Palestine, the Democratic Front for the Liberation of Palestine, the PFLP-General Command, the Iraqi-backed Arab Liberation Front, and the Syrian-operated Saiqa — were opposed. Some charged that the reactionary Saudis were acting in concert with American imperialists to counter progressive revolutionary movements in the region.

The PLO and Superpower Rivalries

The debate over the Fahd plan revealed an interesting paradox: While some Arabs argued that the PLO and the Arab League should withhold support because the plan did not have the firm backing of the United States and therefore stood little chance of being implemented, others rejected it precisely because, they said, it was really an American-backed initiative that would strengthen the pro-Western camp in the region. (Arab rejectionists derisively called it "Camp Fahd.") Thus it could be argued that the more openly the United States endorsed the Fahd plan, the more it would have contributed to polarization in the Arab world.

Arafat, who depended on both Soviet and Saudi support and preferred not to have to choose between them, sought to rebut charges that the two nations were in conflict. In response to such charges by Marxist PDFLP leader Naif Hawatmeh, Arafat declared that "whoever says yes to Brezhnev's plan cannot say no to the Saudi plan." Arafat had gone from Moscow — where he had been received by Brezhnev and where the PLO office had just been raised to embassy status — to Riyadh. He reportedly carried a message from Brezhnev that the Soviet Union was prepared to back the Fahd plan if the Saudis established diplomatic relations with Moscow.

There were indeed some significant points of similarity between the Soviet and Saudi plans. Brezhnev had proclaimed his Peace Program for the 1980s at the 26th Congress of the Communist Party of the Soviet Union on February 23, 1981. Discussing the Middle East, he criticized the United States for organizing "a separate deal beween Egypt and Israel" and proposed that an "all-embracing, just and realistic settlement" be sought in "the framework of a specially convened international conference." In such an effort, the Soviet Union was prepared to act jointly with the United States and other interested parties — "the Arabs (naturally including the Palestine Liberation Organization) and Israel." He also welcomed cooperation by Western Europe and the UN.

The substance of Brezhnev's proposal was that real peace required the end of Israeli occupation "of all Arab territories captured in 1967." He further called for securing the inalienable rights of the Arab people of Palestine "up to and including the establishment of their own state. It is essential to ensure the security and sovereignty of all the states of the region, including those of Israel." Based on these principles, he said, the details could be negotiated. [11]

Since Brezhnev had been far more explicit in recognizing Israel than Fahd, Arafat was asking, in effect, how Hawatmeh could criticize the Saudi plan after having endorsed Moscow's. In an interview with Kuwait's *Al-Ray' Al-'Amm* on November 23, 1981, he replied that Arafat had "embroiled himself in a series of incorrect comparisons." Brezhnev's initiative, Hawatmeh said, was part of "the general struggle against the Camp David Agreements." In other words, Moscow, the rejectionist Arab states and the "progressive" (radical) Palestinian groups had a common interest in undercutting a peace program in which the United States played the key role and from which Washington had successfully excluded the Soviet Union. Moreover, one had to consider the "security and political implications" of Moscow's position because its proposals were offered by "a superpower that defends its political line with all its enormous military, economic and political power." (Hawatmeh was referring to the vast arsenals of arms the Russians were providing for Libya, Iraq and Syria.)

While there was value in winning the support of "a friendly foreign state," Hawatmeh noted that the Soviet Union was nevertheless not "a fraternal Arab state but a foreign state [with] its own policy on this or that international issue." Therefore one should not expect Moscow to see eye-to-eye with the Arabs on every issue; and in any case, its position on recognition of Israel was not binding on the Arabs. (As Professor Galia Golan points out in her paper, the Soviet Union was quite prepared to make abrupt tactical shifts and to treat local Communists in Arab countries as expendable when its national interest dictated good relations with bourgeois regimes it regarded to be nationalist and anti-colonial.)

Hawatmeh proceeded to praise Saudi Arabia for past support of the rights of the Palestinian people, and for going along with earlier Arab summit conferences, including those that had voted sanctions against Egypt for making peace with Israel. He was disturbed that the Saudis were now pushing their own initiative, because when Saudi Arabia proposes a plan and seeks Arab League summit approval for it, he said, "it is defining for the Arabs and the PLO the upper limit of patriotic Arab and Palestinian rights." Specifically, Hawatmeh asked for the elimination of Point 7, which he said proposed recognition of Israel, for removal of five other concessions he claimed to see in the plan, and for insertion of an amendment clearly declaring that the PLO was the sole legitimate representative of the Palestinians. Significantly, such an exclusive PLO designation had been omitted from the Fahd plan, presumably to make it more palatable to the U.S. and the West Europeans, to leave an opening for non-PLO West Bankers, and to let Jordan reassert a role.

All in all, Hawatmeh wanted the Fahd plan transformed from a Saudi initiative to a reaffirmation of the Arab consensus adopted at post-1973 summits from Algiers to Baghdad. He added a veiled warning to Arafat: "It is not the right of any Palestinian leader, irrespective of his rank in the revolution or the PLO, to impose his personal decision on the entire revolution or organization."

The rulers of Libya and Iraq, leaders of the rejectionist camp, refused to attend the Fez summit; but the *coup de grace* was delivered by President Hafez al-Assad of Syria. In addition to the reasons already cited, he was piqued by the Saudis' attempt to assume a major regional role in an issue traditionally regarded by Damascus as concerning Greater Syria. Yet, until the last moment, King Hassan II of Morocco and Crown Prince Fahd of Saudi Arabia thought Assad would come to Fez. Indeed, a Syrian security detail had already arrived, and when Arafat left from the Damascus airport, the presidential plane was being prepared to take off. With Syria absent, and Egypt's delegation barred by the Baghdad sanctions, it was soon clear that debate over the Fahd plan would only exacerbate existing tensions in the Arab world. Officially, King Hassan simply adjourned the summit and the Saudi plan remained on the agenda for future discussion.

Conclusions

Several conclusions can be drawn from this examination of the

PLO and of inter-Arab relations:

1. Neither Saudi Arabia nor any other Arab state can impose its will on the others.

2. Since Arafat could not carry even his own Fatah in support of the Fahd plan, the assumption that he speaks authoritatively for the PLO and can act on behalf of the Palestinians is a great oversimplification.

3. Where there is sharp division within the PLO on any action, the lowest common denominator will be continuation of the hard line of no-coexistence with Israel.

4. Notwithstanding PLO rhetoric of unity, many different factors influence the Palestinians, whose organizational structure, local family ties, economic interests and ideological orientation mirror both the complexity of the surrounding Arab world and broader international currents.

5. While the door must be left open to encourage the Palestinians' participation in the peace process, there will be few practical results until more voices in the Palestinian community and the Arab states are prepared to speak out for recognizing a sovereign State of Israel as a permanent partner in the region.

6. In the formulation of the Arab states' stands on the Palestinian question, mutual suspicion based on particularistic national, ideological, or personal interests still outweighs considerations of broader Arab consensus.

7. These inter-Arab disputes have made it impossible to reach an Arab consensus on solving the Arab-Israel conflict. Today, after the overthrow of the Shah in Iran, the Soviet invasion of Afghanistan, and the Iran-Iraq war, it should be clear that the Palestinian question is by no means the only, or even only major, cause of discord and instability in the region. Those other quarrels have nothing to do with the Arab-Israeli conflict. Indeed, if the militant Palestinians succeeded in achieving their objective of eliminating Israel as a sovereign state, more regional conflicts, a radicalization of the area and the overthrow of pro-Western regimes with geopolitical consequences gravely detrimental to United States interests might well follow.

The conclusion of a report on "The Geopolitics of Oil," issued in November 1980 by the staff of the Senate Committee on Energy

44

and Natural Resources, clearly assessed the impact of intra-regional turmoil on the prospects for peace:

The dispute between Iraq and Iran is only a part of a continuing pattern of local instability and regional conflict. Thirteen of the present Arab heads of state, or more than half, have reached power by forcibly removing their predecessors in one way or another; in the past fifteen years, besides major Arab-Israel conflicts, Arabs have fought Arabs in thirteen fierce wars. While the Egyptian-Israeli peace treaty has contributed significantly to overall stability in the Middle East, systemic problems, exacerbated by the present conflict, will keep the Middle East unstable for the foreseeable future.

Notes

1. *The Nation,* May 9, 1981.

2. Interview with the Kuwait daily, *Al'Ray Al'-Amm,* Dec. 13, 1981, reported in *The Washington Post,* Dec. 14, 1981.

3. Pranay B. Gupte, "Arab Nations: 2 Camps Now," *The New York Times,* Nov. 29, 1980.

4. Loren Jenkins, dispatch from Beirut, *The Washington Post,* Sept. 15, 1981.

5. James Dorsey, *The Christian Science Monitor,* Aug. 5, 1981.

6. Quoted by Dorsey, *ibid.*

7. As far back as December 1973, on the eve of the Geneva peace conference, Sheykh Ahmad Zaki Yamani, the Saudi oil minister, had said on American TV that a comprehensive peace should be based on total Israeli withdrawal from the 1967 occupied territories and the creation of a Palestinian state with East Jerusalem as its capital, in exchange for recognition of Israel by its Arab neighbors. When pressed by "Meet the Press" interviewers as to whether he included Saudi Arabia, Yamani replied, "I don't think we have to," because Saudi Arabia has no common frontier with Israel.

8. Interview with the Kuwait News Agency, published Nov. 25, 1981.

9. *Khaleej Times,* Dubai, Oct. 18, 1981.

10. Agence France Presse, Riyadh, Nov. 21, 1981.

11. English translation from an official pamphlet, *L. I. Brezhnev: Peace Programme for the 80s,* Novosti Press Agency Publishing House, Moscow, 1981, pp. 11-12.

Northern Africa and the Middle East

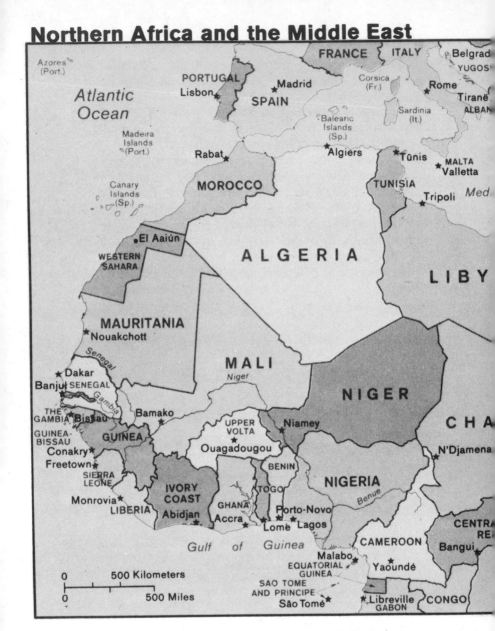

The Middle East and North Africa, cradle of many civilizations, is an area of cultural, social and political diversity — and historic rivalries. It includes 21 independent Arab states spread over 5.3 million square miles, with a total population of 163 million. Eight non-Arab states (Afghanistan, Cyprus, Ethiopia, Greece, Iran, Israel, Turkey and Pakistan), consisting of 226 million people, live in an area of 2 million square miles. Islam is the predominant religion, divided into Sunni and Shi'ite sects. In Cyprus, Ethiopia and Greece, the majority are Christians, as are about half of the

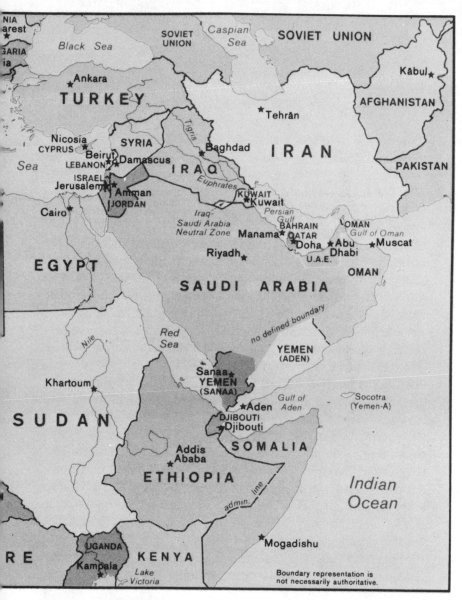

Lebanese; Israel has a Jewish majority. The region includes, in addition to the Palestinians, sizable minority groups of Kurds, Copts, Berbers and various Turkic tribes. The diversity of political organization ranges from the fundamentalist Islamic Republic in Iran and the sheikdoms in the Arabian Peninsula to the constitutional monarchies in Jordan and Morocco and the secular republic of Turkey, and from the one-party military regimes in Libya, Syria and Iraq, to the parliamentary democracies of Israel and Greece.

Yehoshafat Harkabi

THE EVOLUTION OF
THE PALESTINIAN MOVEMENT

It is true, even banal, that political positions are modified by time and changing circumstance. But in analyzing the development of political positions, the important thing is to judge objectively whether or not they have changed, whether they are dynamic or static. The Palestinians have been very consistent in maintaining old positions, often limiting changes to clothing the old ones in new guises and formulations; it is mostly the formal articulation of those positions, and less their substance, that is different.

What characterizes Palestinian positions? What are the contributing factors to their formation? Can we expect substantive change? How may it come about?

Historically, the Palestinian Arabs have not, either sociologically or culturally, been a separate group from the Arabs of the neighboring countries. Nor was Palestine a distinct political entity during the Ottoman period; administratively, it was divided into areas and districts that stretched into adjacent territories. In other words, until recently a Palestinian consciousness could not develop; its impetus came from the outside.

Some Arab leaders in Jerusalem understood quite early that if the Jews were allowed to settle in the country and acquire land, its ethnic character would eventually become Jewish. Therefore, as early as 1891, they petitioned the Ottoman Parliament in Constantinople (Istanbul) to end all Jewish immigration into Palestine — an event one may consider to be the beginning of the Arab-Israeli conflict. The Arabs soon learned of the Zionist movement's aspirations to establish a Jewish majority and create a Jewish haven in Palestine, and it was precisely these aspirations which gave them — especially those who were politically aware — a feeling of distinctness from Arabs who did not live in a region whose political identity was at stake.

However, because Jewish immigration ebbed more than it flowed, this danger did not always seem too grave. Furthermore, such benefits from Jewish immigration as employment, modern health care, technology and, not least, higher land values, muffled a good amount of the resistance against Zionism. In this way, the Palestinian Arabs contributed — actively or by omission — to the building of the Jewish *Yishuv*.

But they also understood immediately the significance of the Balfour Declaration of 1917 and declared their opposition. The "Jewish National Home" in Palestine called for in this British document was ambiguous, not clearly defined either by the British or the Jews; but the Arabs named it *Watan Qaumi,* which literally means a "National Fatherland" and accentuates the political connotation.

In the 1920s, during the first two years of British occupation, the Palestinian Arabs tried to enlist the support of neighboring Arab countries, particularly Syria, in the struggle against the Jewish national home. But they learned quickly that Arabs in these countries gave precedence to their respective national interests and were not ready to exert themselves in the cause of the Palestinians. And several other factors accounted for the lack of coherence and tenacity in the Palestinian Arabs' struggle against Zionism: the people's very limited political awareness, the considerable practical benefits of collaboration with the Jews, a divided leadership whose internecine quarrels overpowered any common effort against Zionism, and the duplicity of these leaders' public protests against the Jews to whom they were privately selling land at ever-mounting prices.

The Palestinian Arabs' political position could be summed up in three demands: an end to Jewish immigration, a prohibition against selling land to Jews (which, in effect, meant demanding that the British Mandatory authorities do what the Arab leaders could neither discipline themselves nor force their people to do), and an independent democratic Palestinian state which would be Arab because of the Arabs' sheer demographic preponderance. This state would legally nip Jewish immigration and the Zionist venture in the bud. In sum, throughout the Mandatory period, prevention — how to thwart Zionist efforts — was the principal ingredient of the Palestinian Arab position.

Israel Becomes a State: The Arabs' Political Position

The UN Partition Plan of 1947, the 1948 war and the establishment of Israel ushered in a new period with new problems. The nature of the Arab-Palestinian positions changed from preventive to restorative, called for a return to the situation in which a Jewish state did not exist. Such an objective required the active destruction of the state or its demise as a political entity, i.e., politicide; but it is generally easier to prevent the establishment of a state than to destroy it once it exists. The universal norm on which world order is based is respect for the existence of states as political bodies, and only changes in political regimes are countenanced. Thus, the Arabs' politicide position collided with a principal international political norm.

It also gave the Palestinian Arab leaders some serious questions to grapple with, for example: Was the destruction of the State of Israel a realistic and feasible objective? How could it be made acceptable to the rest of the world? What programs of action, strategy and tactics were needed to achieve it? How should the Palestinians organize themselves for this purpose? How should they relate to the Arab states and the Arab League, and what price should be paid for their assistance in the struggle? These are still the main questions in the internal Arab debate, so it may be useful to trace the responses over the years, and at the same time look into the historical development of the Palestinian Arab position.

After the 1948 war, the Palestinian Arabs were shattered as a community. The defeat in the war was a bitter shock, for they had believed that with intervention by neighboring Arab armies, they would prevail over the Jewish forces. The old leadership was entirely discredited. The upper classes had fled the country very early in the war, leaving the people leaderless and perplexed.

50

Disintegration and atomization of their society left every individual or family alone, forsaken, to cope with their personal problems. The 1948 defeat deepened the ambivalence which, though it had started earlier, has typified the Palestinians' attitude towards the Arab states: anger and hatred for their deficiencies, and yet dependence on them because of feelings of inadequacy.

At first the Palestinians blamed their exile on the Arab states, whose armies had had to clear away the civilian population to prepare for the coming onslaught. Actually, most of the Palestinians exiled themselves out of fear that they might be caught in the military action; only later in the war did the Israeli army exert pressure in some regions, mostly in order to control a hostile population while military activities were going on.

Pan-Arabism and Nationalist Movements

After 1948, the Palestinians' feeling of weakness led them to expect that a solution of their problems would come through pan-Arab efforts, not their own. Until the late 1950s, the Palestinians evinced little enthusiasm for organizing themselves. Their youth became active in general Arab movements such as *Qaumiun*, Muslim Brotherhood, *Ba'ath*, Communist or Nasserist.[1] Their distinctiveness as Palestinians was accentuated not only by their plight as exiles, but also by their feelings of strangeness in the host Arab states, whose people often treated them as inferiors. Palestinian literature contains many recriminations on this score.

Just as the Jews in Palestine became Israelis, the Palestinian Arabs could assume the name of Palestinians, a distinct community. (There is an irony in the non-Arab character of this appellation, which is derived from Philistine, a non-Semitic people in antiquity.) Significantly, too, the UN Partition Plan of 1947 called for setting up a Jewish state and an *Arab* — not Palestinian — state in the area east of the Jordan River. At the time, Palestine was only a geographic, not an ethnic designation.[2]

The hope of the 1947 refugees to return to an Arab Palestinian state was common among exiles abroad, and was only reinforced by their agony in their new environments. They understood that to achieve their aim, they would have to undo a political fact that had already taken root: the sovereign State of Israel. The call for Israel's demise was at first more a hope than an objective, for they lacked the program or strategy essential to reaching any goal. The Palestinians looked for such a common strategy, but it did not materialize because the Arab states themselves were beset by revolutions and other internal difficulties. Hopes soared in 1958, when it looked as though the Egyptian-Syrian merger had advanced Arab nationalism and unity; but when the United Arab Republic broke up in 1961, hope turned to despair.

The PLO Emerges

Slowly the idea emerged that the Palestinians had to organize themselves into a Palestinian organization in order to lead the struggle and to serve as a nucleus for their future state. After March 1959, these and similar ideas also became an issue of discord and bickering among Arab governments and in Arab League meetings. Finally, in June 1964, the Palestinian Liberation Organization (PLO) was established under Arab League auspices. And since then, whether as object of criticism or of praise and support, the PLO has been at the center of all discussion of Palestinian policy.

At the same time, the Palestinians started to organize themselves in clandestine organizations. Thus the nucleus of the most important of such groups, Fatah, first started its activities in the ideological field in Kuwait in 1959. It began its military activities in 1965 from bases in Syria as an opposition group to the PLO.

In September 1963, by a somewhat fortuitous turn of events, Ahmad Shuqayri (later the founder of the PLO) became the Palestine representative in the Arab League, a post that had existed in various forms since the League's establishment in 1945. Faced with a situation in which the Palestinians were being torn by different ideologies and factions, Shuqayri wanted to unite them in one organization; but first he had to create a program or platform to which all of them would agree. He labored very hard to formulate a draft of the Palestinian Covenant and submitted it to Arab governments — first to the Jordanians, whom he wanted to assure that the proposed organization was not detrimental to their interests, then to the Palestinians themselves to enlist their participation. On the basis of this draft, the first constitutive Palestinian National Council was convened in East Jerusalem, then under Jordan's control, where the Covenant was promulgated on June 2, 1964 and became basic doctrine. In other words, the Covenant preceded the PLO and was, in fact, the basis for its creation. The June meeting became the First Palestinian National Council (PNC), the highest PLO authority and its legislative body.

At the end of 1967, Shuqayri was blamed for alienating world opinion, which supported Israel in the Six Day War, and was ousted from the PLO chairmanship. The PLO changed its organization in order to accommodate the *fedayeen* groups which had theretofore opposed it.[3] In July 1968, the fourth PNC amended the Covenant, and because the amendments did not change its nature and main characteristics, we can look at the two versions together.

The Palestinian Covenant

I recently analyzed the Palestinian Covenant in the Introduction to *The Palestinian Covenant and Its Meaning* (Vallentine Mitchell: London, 1979), and perhaps the following revised passages can serve as a summary:

The Palestinian Covenant's central tenet is a total repudiation of Israel's existence; this stand, and its theoretical and practical implications, have been institutionalized in an ideological system. The claim that Israel should not exist is implicit in almost half of the 33 articles (1961 version), including those formulated as definitions and axioms; the demand for Israel's demise becomes inevitable necessity by definition, a kind of scientific truth. Israel must cease to exist not so much because that is in the Palestinians' interest, but because its disappearance is implicit in the definition of Palestinism as an attribute of both a people and a country. Palestine is the Palestinians' homeland which must not be separated from the Arab world, and the Palestinians are an integral part of the Arab nation. The *whole* of Palestine must be returned to them and placed under their sovereignty, because only in all of Palestine can they realize self-determination, redeem themselves from alienation, and regain dignity and freedom. The corollary to this concept is the theory — also formulated as definitional truth — that the Jews are not a nation and therefore, in principle, neither deserve a state of their own nor, as a non-nation, are able to maintain it.

Zionism is condemned not only because it is "racist" and linked to imperialism, but because its evil deeds flow from its very essence. To abolish Israel would be not only legal, but also beneficial to the Palestinians, the Arabs and humanity in general. The Covenant thus encompasses intrinsic moral, utilitarian, volitional, legal and historical arguments, all of which converge into total repudiation, on principle, of the existence of the State of Israel in any form or size.

The Palestinian movement claims absoluteness and "totalism," an unqualified Manichaean division of good and evil: There is absolute justice in Palestinian claims, absolute injustice in Israel's; right is only on the Palestinians' side; only they are worthy of self-determination. The Jews in Israel are barely human creatures who, at best, may be tolerated in a Palestinian state as individuals or as a religious community, with their numbers effectively reduced to some 5 percent of their present total in the area and then absorbed into the Arab environment. (This figure is based on Article 6 in the 1968 amended Covenant, which would accept Jews who resided in Palestine in 1917 and their offspring, and exclude later immigrants.) The historical link of the Jews to the land of Israel is presented as deceit, the spiritual link — the centrality of the land of Israel to Judaism — as fraud. Such international decisions as the League of Nations Mandate in 1922 and the United Nations Partition Plan in 1947 are rejected out of hand.

Throughout the conflict, Arab spokesmen have toiled to clothe the intent to liquidate Israel in positive slogans: "the liberation of Palestine," "return," "realization of self-determination for the Palestinians," "a just solution," "the establishment of a democratic state," and so on. The tendency is to avoid saying explicitly that realization of such goals presupposes the liquidation of Israel as a political entity, that is, to speak positively about what they seek to accomplish and to ignore the negative by-products. The Palestinians' right to self-determination becomes their right to self-definition in a way that excludes the possibility of Israel's existence. In other words, self-determination becomes permission to determine that Israel shall not be. Arab and Palestinian spokesmen disclaim the intention to "destroy" Israel, indeed

54

probably hope that its physical assets — buildings, industry and so on — will remain after they conquer it. However, this is a quibble; the destruction of Israel means its liquidation as a political entity.

Notwithstanding its blatant anti-Israeli substance, the Palestinian Covenant is a sophisticated document that does not use terms like "liquidation of Israel"; the closest expressions are "elimination of Zionism in Palestine" (Article 15), and an assertion that the establishment of Israel is "entirely illegal, regardless of the passage of time" (Article 19). The magic incantation by many commentators that Arab extremism is merely a display of emotion that should not be taken at face value cannot apply to such a meticulously drafted and polished doctrinal document as the Palestinian Covenant. Its rejection of Israel is neither an emotional outburst nor a rhetorical expedient; it is a thoroughly contrived political conception, a carefully worked out doctrine with a well constructed ideology. It is not blind hatred but reasoned hostility, not only on the affective but also on the cognitive level.

Although the central theme of the Covenant is absolute refusal to coexist with Israel, the possibility cannot be discarded that one day the PLO will reverse its rejectionist position and accept coexistence. Nevertheless, one should beware of treating this possible outcome as though it had already occurred, simply out of hope or out of conviction that it is inevitable. No national document is a commitment that cannot be rescinded; and the Covenant could be modified officially by two-thirds vote in a special meeting of the Palestine National Council, the legislature of the PLO, if it wished. Furthermore, Fatah commands the majority of votes in the PNC, and it is significant that it does not use its numerical preponderance to amend or change the Covenant. And it might be abrogated *de facto* through systematic avoidance of any mention or reference to it, which could be a sign that it had been consigned to oblivion; but actually, the opposite was happening until lately, and the number of references to the hallowed Covenant has increased in PNC resolutions. So the absence of reference to the Covenant was one of the novelties in the 15th PNC of April 1981, but it is too early to judge if it signifies a trend.

Ever since its content has been known to world public opinion, the Covenant with its absolutist position of non-coexistence with

Israel has done considerable damage to the Palestinian cause; even some Palestinian voices have called for its modification. Furthermore, the PLO wants nothing more than U.S. recognition, which is conditioned on its modifying the Covenant and accepting, in principle, Israel's existence. Therefore, if the PLO does not accept Israel — acceptance being tantamount to discarding the Covenant's uncompromising stand — there must be very weighty reasons why. They deserve examination.

Why the PLO Refuses to Change the Basic Tenets of the Covenant

The Cohesive Function: The Covenant, which embodies the basic Palestinian positions, is the bond uniting all PLO factions. Important circles within the PLO hold tenaciously to the idea of non-coexistence with Israel, whatever the price or however long it takes to realize the absolute objective. A shift to coexistence with Israel might result in a split in the PLO and a ferocious internal struggle; discord between factions in the past has already resulted in fratricidal showdowns with more casualties than clashes with Israel. No wonder the common urge is to prevent internecine war.

The Constitutional Imperative: When the PNC chose Shuqayri as leader, he was authorized to appoint the members of the Executive Committee — the PLO Cabinet or Directorate. But since the fourth PNC in July 1968, the PNC has been choosing the members of this committee, which now represents the various factions or *fedayeen* groups within the PLO, and which appoints its chairman — currently Yasir Arafat — who serves as the official overall leader. Therefore, although Arafat has great power because his Fatah group is by far the largest and most important in the PLO, he has less authority than Shuqayri had. The movement is less tightly knit, and every faction possesses some power to veto change, which strengthens the tendency to hold fast to old positions. This plurality of organizations moves the PLO toward more rigid stands, whose common denominator leans toward those of the extreme *fedayeen* groups.

The *fedayeen* organizations have changed, some splitting into several mutually inimical groups, some disappearing altogether. At present there are six with representation in the PNC and the Executive Committee: Fatah, the largest and most important, which makes it a point to avoid social ideology in order to maintain relations with all Arab states; Saiqa, established by the Syrian Ba'ath Party and subservient to the Syrian Government; PFLP the Popular Front for the Liberation of Palestine, led by Dr. George Habash, whose ill health limited his personal activity for several years until recently, when he returned to his place on the Executive Committee; PDFLP the Popular Democratic Front for the Liberation of Palestine, led by Naif Hawatmeh and the closest to the Soviets; the Arab Liberation Front, established by Iraqi Ba'ath leader Abd al-Kahim Ahmad; and the PFLP-General Command, led by Ahmad Jibril, which split from PFLP and is close to the Syrians. Two smaller groups represented only in the PNC are the Popular Struggle Front led by Dr. Samir Ghosha, and the Liberation of Palestine Front, led by Abu al-Abas, which split from Jibril's organization in April 1977. In April 1981, at the latest PNC — the 15th — Dr. Habash's PFLP returned after an absence of eight years to the Executive Committee (although it had retained membership in the PNC). This development may strengthen the opposition to any change in basic PLO positions.

Practical Considerations: Acceptance of coexistence with Israel would mean that the PLO would have to consider the West Bank and Gaza to be the maximum, final Palestinian share of Palestine west of the Jordan River. (Even a Labor government in Israel might insist on some adjustment of the borders existing before the Six Day War.) Such a settlement might satisfy the present inhabitants of those areas and some of their leaders — the mayors of the Arab towns, for example — but it would confront Palestinians elsewhere with some painful problems: what to do with the Palestinians in Lebanon, for instance, since the existence of a Palestinian state would increase Lebanese pressure to send them there.

Furthermore, the Palestinians in Lebanon are the main constituency of the PLO leadership, and the best organized, most active group of their kind in the world. A mini-state in the West Bank is no solution for their problems, and it is no wonder that the idea is not popular with them.

Another thorny problem would be the relationship of such a state with Jordan. Territorially, Jordan might be its link to the other Arab countries, but that would give Jordan considerable leverage over the new state. The Palestinian Arabs in Jordan, about 50 percent of the country's total population, would have to decide whether they are Jordanians or Palestinians; their present ambivalence would have to end. They would probably choose Jordan, for in recent years many Palestinians have been "Jordanized"; but Jordan has not been Palestinized.

Some Fundamental Issues: Generally, the Arabs define their identity ethnically, culturally and linguistically; an Arab is someone who speaks Arabic. But the Palestinians define themselves territorially as the people who live in or came from Palestine, so to agree to a smaller Palestine might be like amputating their identity. They feel they are the people of all of Palestine, not of a small Palestine.

The PLO is literally a movement for liberation of Palestine in its "entirety," an expression that recurs again and again in its resolutions. It is not the PPLO, the "Part-of-Palestine Liberation Organization." To resign themselves to the idea that the PLO is only a PPLO would be a most fundamental and radical change in the Palestinians' ideology and self-image.

But King Hussein has not given up hope to control the West Bank, which he considers to be a lesser evil than an independent Palestinian state that would undoubtedly try to subvert his regime. However, he does not consider it a practical proposition at present, especially since a claim to that territory could only do him harm. So he bides his time.

A Palestinian state on the West Bank would spell the end of the PLO's heroic period and its important role on the international scene; it would, in Arafat's expression, be a demotion to the status of "village leaders." PLO leaders probably would not want to bother with the prosaic problems of daily life in a state; they would engage in a cruel struggle for power and compete with local West Bank leaders. The great dependence of a small state on other Arab nations would be incompatible with the Palestinians' passion for independence.

Further, a settlement with Israel would entail such obligations as stopping all violence against the former enemy and making political arrangements to ensure the peace — a not very attractive job for former Palestinian freedom fighters. Israel would be able to

58

exert pressure on the new state with its military force and through control of the road from the West Bank to Gaza.

These problems, although not insoluble, weigh heavily against any PLO tendency to change its basic course of action. On the other hand, the organization will have to adapt to developments in the international arena.

How Moderate Is the PLO Today?

The Palestinian National Covenant was amended only once — in July 1968 — and those changes merely accentuated the impetus toward self-reliance and incorporated the doctrine of "armed struggle." It also added a limitation on the number of Jews allowed to live in the Liberated Palestine, which would reduce the Jewish population of Israel to a small fraction of its present size. In sum, the PLO position was radicalized in the 1968 version of the Covenant.

In March 1971, to counterbalance the effect of this radical stand, the eighth PNC said the Palestinian objective was to set up a secular democratic state in which Jews and Palestinian Arabs would live together in peace. However, the basic political position of the PLO was not changed; its readiness to live with Jews meant unreadiness to live with their state. Nor did the PNC specify how the democratic state could be achieved, for the PLO clung to the idea of "return"; and if all Palestinians who wished to were allowed to return to the country and recover their landed property, a large proportion of the Jewish population would have to be evicted from their homes. So, the PLO's democratic-state slogan did not have the desired effect of making its objectives appear moderate.

Nevertheless, the organization was making very considerable headway in the international arena; in 1974 the PLO was recognized by the UN General Assembly. Two factors converged to help make it possible: First, the Arab states were growing more important in the world — in numbers, in control of oil, in strategic position. And second, the PLO was riding a historical wave; self-determination had become a generally accepted norm.

The PLO claims this right to self-determination even as it refuses to recognize that Israelis have it too. And scandalous as it may seem, world public opinion has not insisted on this reprocity as a condition for granting the Palestinians their right to self-determination. Perhaps Israeli diplomacy, too, might have pressed more adeptly for it. One may surmise that if Israel, when these questions were debated in the UN, had agreed to some recognition of Palestinian rights, even in the version subsequently accepted in the Camp David Accords, if Israel had suggested a reciprocity formula to the General Assembly, and if Israel's right to self-determination had been included in the UN resolutions, the PLO might, at the least, have had second thoughts on the advisability of pressing for its own self-determination. Israel's official stand would have had to change, but the PLO's far more so, for reciprocity — both sides enjoying the same right to self-determination — contradicts the PLO's fundamental tenets.

There are those who argue that the PLO's terrorist operations attracted world attention to its grievances and were instrumental in its international achievements. The argument is an exaggeration, for without the other two factors in its favor — the support of Arab states and the norm of self-determination — PLO terrorism would not have accomplished much. Operationally, and especially in relation to Israel, its military achievements have, in fact, been quite limited.

The 1973 war ushered in a new era in the Arab-Israeli conflict, prompting a movement for settlement, first in the form of agreements for the separation of armed forces, and culminating in the Camp David negotiations and the peace treaty with Egypt. The PLO had to adjust itself to the new political climate — no easy task, since it was unwilling to abandon its basic position. However, the 12th PNC in June 1974 found a formula which expressed readiness to accept a Palestinian "authority" in any area evacuated by Israel, provided it did not mean peace or giving up the basic tenet of regaining the whole of Palestine. In the 13th PNC, this "authority" was called a "state" — a convenient tactical device, an interim step or phase which did not entail forgoing that basic claim. Recently the formula has become acceptable to all PLO factions — including the PFLP which at first opposed it — precisely because it does not close the door to the PLO's continued struggle for the fundamental objective.

That position has been reiterated in subsequent PNC meetings and is now the official PLO stand, which stresses the centrality of the Palestinians to the conflict, their agony, their need for a state, and the PLO's status as their sole representative. However, the formula is careful not to go farther, that is, it does not declare explicitly that the establishment of a state would end the conflict and that the PLO would then be ready to live in peace and in good neighborly relations with Israel. The stress is on guarantees for this political arrangement by the big powers, which means that the Palestinians themselves would be free of specific obligations concerning Israel.

Khalid al-Hasan, a member of the Fatah Central Committee and the chairman of the PNC Foreign Relations Committee, recently summed up the current PLO position in the PLO monthly, *Shu'un Filastiniyya:* "After the 1973 war and the understanding of its consequences, the Palestinian leadership and the Palestinian National Council have adopted the idea of phasing (*marhaliyya*) in the program of the Palestinian struggle, and thus agreed to a Palestinian independent state on any liberated part of the Palestinian territory, provided it does not entail any condition preventing the realization of its final goals." Earlier in the article, al-Hasan, who is regarded as a moderate within the PLO, reiterated that "the final goal is the establishment of the Palestinian Democratic state in the entirety of Palestine."[4]

Furthermore, if PLO formulations have become more flexible, they have been more than balanced by a stiffer emphasis on the principle of "return" as a major tenet in both ideology and program, which would guarantee that adherence to the basic objective does not erode. And the PLO means collective, not individual return.

Camp David and After

The Camp David agreement specified that Palestinian autonomy in the West Bank and Gaza would last for several years until the final form of West Bank government had been decided. There is some divergence of opinion on the significance or implications of this modality: Presumably Presidents Sadat and Carter considered that autonomy was a first installment in the settlement, that its implementation would develop to virtual Arab independence in the area or something close to it. Mr. Begin, on the other hand, thinks autonomy is the last installment, and that it will enable Israel to control the West Bank even if many functions of self-rule have been passed to the Arab inhabitants. Strange as it may seem, the PLO takes Mr. Begin as its mentor on the meaning of Camp David, and uses his interpretation to justify rejection of Palestinian participation in negotiations with Israel toward a political settlement.

Because the PLO cannot use the Jordanian and Syrian areas as a springboard, the West Bank has become the main arena of confrontation with Israel. Activity from Lebanon has become limited, so that every clash on the West Bank between students and Israeli soldiers, however insignificant, is immediately covered by the press throughout the world.

Palestinians on the West Bank will acknowledge that the PLO is their sole representative, but there is reason to suspect that there are latent divergent interests among their present leaders. West Bank leaders are not eager to surrender their positions to PLO people from the outside, which is what happened in Algeria when outsiders like Ben Bella and Boumedienne seized power. [5]

From time to time, more moderate Palestinian voices refer to an eventual readiness to coexist with Israel, and there is undoubtedly an ongoing debate on this question. Apparently, the majority still cling to the old hard line and stamp their mark of approval on the PLO's corporate position. As individuals, PLO moderates argue that by clinging to that stand, the Palestinians may forfeit their chances to participate in the negotiations; but these apparent moderates are not an organized group, which of course limits their influence.

Thus, the general attitude towards a Palestinian mini-state is ambivalent: On the one hand, there are apprehensions that it will block the way to an all-Palestine objective, and on the other, there is a feeling that such a state is a necessary, even inevitable step toward reaching the full objective, and that this ultimate goal is worth a few concessions.

Journalists, including some Israelis, repeatedly publish scoops that the PLO is on the verge of changing its basic no-coexistence stand. So far, all such revelations have been denied, usually the next day, by the sources to which the journalists referred or by the PLO central office. What all these oscillations serve to prove is that such a step would be very difficult for the PLO.

It is repeatedly argued that the PLO is ready to change its position on coexistence and recognition of Israel, but postpones such a démarche or concession until eventual negotiations, where it can be used as the highest trump. The argument is false, for nothing has served Israel better than the PLO's rejection of coexistence; it is the PLO that needs to change its stand, not Israel.

To describe the basic attitudes of Israel and the Palestinians — or the PLO, their representative — as symmetrical is a travesty of truth. For example, Israel took an important step by recognizing, in the Camp David agreement, "the legitimate rights of the Palestinian people," but reciprocal recognition of Israel is still anathema to the leaders of the PLO.

A concluding remark. My personal position is that Israel must follow a moderate course. I do not doubt that most Palestinians consider the PLO to be their representative. I acknowledge that as an organized political group with group consciousness, the Palestinians deserve self-determination — which ultimately means political expression in a state. And I think it will come one day. But I hear no evidence that the PLO has changed its position. Let us beware of being history's cosmeticians of political reality. Yes, it is important that Israel change its position on the PLO, but that is not really the main obstacle to the PLO's changing its own. Indeed, the PLO has shown no readiness to live in peace with Israel or to normalize relations. And yet it is important that Israel take a moderate stand and pass the onus of proof completely to the PLO. At the same time, we have to differentiate between a diplomatic stance, which can be changed by negotiation, and a rigid national position. The PLO's rejection of Israel's existence is not a diplomatic, but a basic national stand. It is simply unrealistic to demand that Israel recognize the PLO, and then trust that it will change one of its basic national tenets through negotiation later on.

Notes

1. *Qaumiun,* the Arab Nationalist Movement created mostly by students in the American University of Beirut who cherished Pan-Arab aspirations, spread to other Arab countries. The Popular Front for the Liberation of Palestine of Dr. Habash developed from its ranks. *Ba'ath,* an ideological movement which centers on a pan-Arab ideology, developed in Syria. In different versions, it is the official ideology in present-day Syria and Iraq.

2. Indeed the original "Palestine Mandate" assigned to Great Britain by the League of Nations had included Transjordan. The area on the East Bank, comprising some four-fifths of the total area of Mandatory Palestine, had been turned over by Britain to Emir Abdullah, who had become King in 1946 when the British unilaterally granted independence to the Hashemite Kingdom of Jordan.

3. *Fedayeen* is the name commonly used in Arabic to denote irregulars who act against Israel. The word comes from the root "sacrifice," i.e., those who sacrifice themselves or assume a suicidal mission. Historically, the name Assassins was given in the twelfth century to those selected to assassinate the enemies of the Isma'ili sect.

4. *Shu'un Filastiniyya,* Nos. 122-123 (Jan-Feb. 1982), p. 42 and p. 41. The Arabic original uses the term *marhaliyya* to describe the tactical approach of implementing the Palestinian objective in phases or stages.

5. In an effort to counter PLO and Jordanian influence on the West Bank and to create a nucleus of local Arabs who may be prepared to cooperate in the Self-Governing Authority projected under the Camp David Accords, Israel has been encouraging the formation of Village Leagues among the two-thirds of the Palestinian population who are rural, and providing them with aid and services. The PLO has responded by assassinating Village League officials — some 17 were killed over the past year. Jordan responded by issuing an official order, on March 9, 1982, threatening that any Palestinian who does not withdraw from Israeli-supported organizations within one month "will be prosecuted for treason" and subject to a maximum penalty of death and confiscation of all property. — *Editor.*

Daniel J. Elazar

ISRAELI ATTITUDES TO
THE PALESTINIANS

The views of Israeli Jews regarding the Palestinian Arabs are
hardly monolithic, but whatever their diversity, all flow out of a
common wish and a general ambivalence. The common wish of
virtually all Israelis is that the Palestinians would simply go away. It
is possible to get many Israelis to articulate this wish when they are
pushed to do so, but needless to say, its very unreality means that it
is rarely articulated and, if articulated, it is rapidly dismissed from
consideration. Yet it should be noted at the outset, because for
Israeli Jews, every other option, no matter which they choose, is
clearly a poor second.

If it existed without the fundamental ambivalence, then one
might even conclude that there is a certain symmetry between that
wish and the Palestinians' fervent desire to be rid of the Israelis. But
it is the ambivalence that makes the difference. Most Israelis can
sympathize with the Palestinian Arabs as human beings — and do
— even if they cannot take the steps that even moderate Palestinians
view as necessary to solve their national problem. Unfortunately,
the Palestinians do not seem to be able to feel the same vis-à-vis the
Jews of Israel.

It has often been remarked that there is a notable lack of hatred
toward the Arabs on the part of the Israeli population as a whole.
This assessment remains true, although it, too, is laced with certain
ambivalences. Most expressions of hatred come from teenagers, a
group not generally noted for its sensitivity and, in Israel, one for
whom Arab hostility is a matter of life and death. It has been
claimed that the Jews who originally came from Arab countries

65

harbor greater hostility toward the Arabs than those who did not. In fact, there, too, feelings are ambivalent. On the one hand, there are those who bitterly recall — or have learned about it from their parents — the hostile attitudes and behavior of Arabs toward the Jews in their midst. At the same time, however, there is on some level a certain cultural kinship that moderates antagonistic feelings. Similarly, it has been suggested that Israeli Jews of European or American background have fewer negative feelings toward the Arabs. This seems to be true on the political level, but they also seem to have a certain very real distaste for Arab culture, which they consider to be foreign and unappealing.

Needless to say, the biggest ambivalence of all is not in the Israeli Jews' recognition of the Palestinian Arabs' humanity—that is not a problem — but in the Israelis' perception of the reality of Palestinian existence and the legitimacy of the Palestinians' search for a place in the sun. The Israeli Jews correctly perceive that the Palestinian Arabs as a group are an uncompromising element, sworn to the elimination of Israel and its Jewish population however much they may sugarcoat the issue for political purposes. The Jews see the Palestinians as a group that is not prepared to recognize reality and to share in a land which now contains two peoples, whatever the historic situation may have been in the immediate past.

Most Israelis are also ambivalent about the fact that, as Jews, they do not like the role of conqueror, occupier, suppressor of a national movement, or whatever, but as Israelis they must be concerned with their security vis-à-vis an apparently implacable foe. This view is widely shared in Israel; it is as much a part of the outlook of those most committed to maximum concessions to the Arabs as of that of the "hardliners." Only their efforts to deal with the problem are different.

If Israeli policy towards the Palestinian Arabs and the territories in which they reside has not always been clear-cut — and indeed it has not — that is a reflection of the depth of the ambivalences among Israeli Jews, which affect the highest governmental circles as well as the person in the street. Often these ambivalences have been a paralyzing factor in Israeli policy-making (at least before the Begin government), a factor that has been brought no nearer to resolution by the actions of the Palestinians themselves.

66

Beyond these shared ambivalences, there are three historic approaches to the problem of the Arabs in the Land of Israel which, while no longer tenable in view of developments since 1967, have strongly influenced the thinking of policy makers in the past and continue to do so today. We will explore the three historic positions, their collapse, and the resulting situation since 1967.

The Zionist Vision: Three Interpretations

It has often been suggested that the original Zionists utterly ignored the Arabs in their eager pursuit of Jewish national revival in the ancient homeland. At the very best, this is a great oversimplification, and in most respects it is simply not true. With a few exceptions, all the early Zionist leaders make clear reference to the indigenous population, and many even suggest directly or obliquely what the relations between the returning Jews and the indigenously settled Arabs should be. What the Zionist movement failed to note — again with few exceptions — was Arab nationalism, which was developing parallel to Jewish nationalism. As 19th-century Europeans, the Zionists saw the indigenous population as essentially passive. Indeed, beginning with Herzl if not before, they saw the Zionist enterprise as taking the Arabs as individuals out of backwardness and passivity, and elevating them to an active role in the new Jewish society. Herzl provides the classic model of this view in his utopian novel *Altneuland*.

It was not until the 1920s, when the facts of Arab nationalism were brutally brought home to the Jews in Palestine and to the Zionist movement, that any effort was made to revise Zionist thinking. Indeed it is one of the tragedies of the history of the Zionist enterprise that the leaders who negotiated the beginnings of the Jewish national home in Palestine after the Balfour Declaration and the British conquest of the land during World War I were so utterly unaware of the national aspirations of the indigenous Arabs that they preferred to leave dealing with them to the British. They did so against the advice of the indigenous Jewish notables, mostly of Sephardic background, who had governed the Jewish community for centuries under the Turks, who knew their Arab neighbors and understood what was happening. For obvious reasons, the Zionists were quite willing to recognize Arab nationalism in other

67

parts of the Middle East, simply hoping that an undivided Arab nationalism would be willing to compromise with Jewish aspirations in Palestine, at least west of the Jordan River.

By the time the local expressions of the national spirit began to have an impact, the Palestinian Arabs had already adopted intractable positions from which they have never receded. The Jewish response at that point was reasonable enough, suggesting that since the Palestinian Arabs were espousing Arab nationalism and not a separate Palestinian nationalism, they should find their satisfaction in the vast territories of the Arab world, leaving the mere 10,000 square miles of western Palestine for the Jews. (By that time eastern Palestine had been detached from the Jewish national home, renamed Transjordan and launched on the road to becoming Jordan.) The indigenous Arab inhabitants would remain as a cultural community rather than as a national collectivity.

What is notable about the early Zionist consideration of the Arabs is that while it may have been tainted with colonialist ideas of native expectations, it was not colonialist in character. Rather, it looked upon the Arabs as potential citizens, not as hewers of wood and drawers of water. The various ideas advanced by Zionist leaders and thinkers, and even by ordinary settlers (if such a distinction can be made, given the strong intellectual and ideational equipment which individual settlers brought with them),addressed the issue of how to bring the Arabs into the new Jewish society on an appropriately humane and egalitarian basis. Three general positions were developed in response to this question, one by the Labor or Socialist camp, one by the Revisionists and Liberals (or what, in Israel, became known as the civil camp), and one by the religious camp.

Labor Prepares the Way for Partition

By and large, it may be said that the Labor group's position was separationist or partitionist in character, for reasons originally having nothing to do with the Arabs.[1] Labor sought the development of a separate Jewish society in the land. Its interest was in transforming what its members saw as the unnatural character of Diaspora Jewry into a more natural socioeconomic order in which Jews attained self-fulfillment through their own agricultural and manual labor rather than by exploiting (in the socialist sense) the labor of others. This classic socialist position led its original exponents, members of the Second Aliyah (1904-13) and Third Aliyah (1919-23), to engage in bitter battles with the Jewish settlers who had preceded them in the country over the employment of cheap Arab labor on their farms in place of Jewish labor. Ultimately Labor was impelled to develop its own institutions, from agricultural settlements to industrial and commercial enterprises, within the framework of what later became the Histadrut.

In their effort to build a society of Jewish workers, the Labor Zionists simply excluded the Arabs without any intended malice. They had no design to diminish the Arabs' economic opportunities; the Arabs simply did not fit into their scheme. Thus the Labor parties and their members became separationists and partitionists long before partition became a political option. While there was a very serious struggle among the Labor Zionists over whether or not to accept the partition of western Palestine, in fact it was relatively easy for them to do so when the time came because their major goal was to build a separate Jewish society on socialist principles. For most Labor Zionists, this goal was more important than the territorial integrity of the country, especially in light of other considerations, such as the desire for a politically sovereign Jewish state of any reasonable size, in control of its own immigration policy in order to save the Jews of Europe.

Since Labor became dominant in the late 1920s and early 1930s, it led the way to partition in 1947-48. In the late stages of Israel's war of independence, when its generals urged Ben Gurion to utilize the by-then superior Israeli military power to extend the borders of the new state into what is now the West Bank and the Gaza Strip, Ben Gurion held back, principally because he feared the opposition of the Western powers, but also because he did not want to absorb the Arabs in these territories (by that time Arabs were no longer fleeing from the Jews). A secure Jewish majority was obviously more important to him than territory.

This position continued to be held by veteran Labor figures all the way through the post-1967 period, but it encountered two major problems. First, while a Jewish majority materialized after 1948 in Israel and indeed became very substantial, the Labor commonwealth collapsed both as an idea and a reality. The mass influx of Jews did not bring committed socialist pioneers; quite the contrary. Moreover, socialism in Israel showed the same deficiencies as elsewhere, and even the socialist leadership of the country had to modify its policies drastically to cope with new realities.

As Israel moved from socialism to social democracy with an increasingly capitalist base (including state capitalism), a major portion of the underpinnings of the old Labor argument for Jewish-Arab separation diminished. Thus, after the Six Day War changed the map of Israel, the second generation of leaders in the Labor Zionist camp, dominated by Moshe Dayan and Shimon Peres, were not moved by the old partitionist considerations. While they shared the general Jewish ambivalence about accepting a large Arab minority with a high birth rate, they also saw the necessity (and wanted) to maintain a Jewish presence in the occupied territories. Looking for a compromise between outright annexation and repartition — they supported a "functional solution," a form of shared rule. Thus they turned a major segment of the Labor group away from partitionist thinking as simply no longer practical. Only Yigal Allon tried to find a new basis for a repartition that would solve Israel's security needs, but even he, in his last years, came to the conclusion that simple partition was no longer possible. [2]

What characterized men like Allon and Dayan, natives of Israel, was that they had developed serious personal relations with their Arab neighbors. Thus their attitude towards the Palestinians was one of openness, a readiness for friendship on an individual basis. Yet, they showed the same ambivalence as their fellow Israelis with regard to the precise relationship that should develop between the two groups.

The collapse of Labor's solid partitionist position in the face of internal dissension and the abandonment of that position by the post-1967 Labor governments did not, to all intents and purposes, lead to the creation of a new policy but rather to political paralysis. The party was too divided to take a firm stand in any direction. Its diffidence was reinforced by Arab intransigence, which led to the Palestinians' rejection of even the tentative solutions the Labor government frequently put forward. Only after the Likud assumed power did a majority of Labor coalesce around a repartition scheme of some kind. Peres, by then the party's leader, adopted this position, probably for tactical purposes and with no great conviction. In the meantime, new military technology has so transformed the security situation that repartition of the territory west of the Jordan becomes increasingly difficult for Israel.

The Civil Camp Champions Integration and Equal Rights

If the Labor group had its reasons for falling into a partitionist position, the Revisionists and the Liberals had theirs for adopting an integrationist stance. For them, too, it was a matter of combining idealism and self-interest. The original farmers of the First Aliyah (1880-1895) and their heirs, as well as many Jews in the urban areas, employed Arab labor as a matter of course, for economic advantage. They opposed the demands of the socialist Zionists to employ Jewish labor exclusively and hence became economic integrationists willy-nilly, although like all other Jews and Arabs, they saw the two peoples as otherwise maintaining national and cultural separation.

On the other hand, the Revisionists envisioned a unified state of Arabs and Jews, with equal rights for both, as the basis for maintaining the unity of Eretz Israel. As 19th-century nationalists, they were committed to a Jewish state in all of historic Eretz Israel, and as 19th-century liberal democrats they could not justify such a state even in their own minds unless all its citizens had equal rights. That is why they emphasized the rapid creation of a Jewish majority in the country through mass immigration, so that the extension of civil rights to Jews and Arabs alike would not interfere with the building of a Jewish national home. This principle was so important to them that it became part of their party anthem whose central theme is a Jewish state on both banks of the Jordan, a state in which Arabs and Jews, Muslims and Christians are all equal citizens.

The Herut Party, the heirs of the Revisionists and the dominant element in the Likud, has remained thoroughly consistent in its commitment to this position. It is expressed in Menachem Begin's proposal of autonomy as a prelude to full Israeli absorption of the West Bank on the basis of civil equality for its Arab inhabitants. Begin said as much in his original proposal of December 1977, a month after Anwar Sadat's visit to Jerusalem, and he and his supporters have reiterated this position regularly, whenever they deem it appropriate.

The integrationist position foundered on the rock of Arab nationalism. The Arabs wanted no part of equal rights in a state with a Jewish majority; they wanted to maintain their Arab majority and keep the Jews out. They did not accept the Revisionist position in the past, and they do not accept it today. The Likud government presses on with its absorption policies and finds no takers among the Palestinian Arabs who live beyond the 1949 armistice lines.

The Religious Community Ignores the Arabs

By and large, the characteristic position of the religious community was to ignore the Palestinian Arabs altogether. Preoccupied as its members were with forging a place for themselves within the Zionist movement or with bringing Zionism into the sphere of religiously sanctioned behavior, they found little to say about the Arabs, except when circumstances brought them in contact with them and improvised responses prevailed. Otherwise, the religious socialists followed the general position of the Labor group, and the non-socialist religious Zionists went along with the civil camp.

Unconcern was a tenable stance as long as the religious community did not have to deal with the Arab problem in other than an ad hoc way, and that did not happen until after 1967. The arguments over partition in the 1930s and 1940s centered around the question of whether to insist on all of historic Palestine or to compromise in order to get at least some kind of Jewish state. The Arab question barely figured. Between 1948 and 1967, the religious community, like the other political groups, rarely had any relations with the Arab minority in the country (except in pre-election negotiations between political leaders).

A radical transformation occurred after 1967, as the members of the religious community came into more contact with the Palestinian Arabs in the administered territories than any other segment of the Jewish population. This contact has assumed many forms. Members of the religious camp led settlement efforts on the West Bank. First they reestablished the former Religious Zionist settlements of the Etzion Bloc that had existed before 1948. Finally there were the efforts of Gush Emunim (a predominantly — but not exclusively — religious faction) to extend Jewish settlement into

72

every part of the administered territories. And day-to-day contact of an intense kind takes place in Jerusalem, where religious Jews, even more than others, are attracted to the Western Wall and to other places of historic and religious association in the Old City.

Through the participation of the religious elements in these activities, by way of actual implantation of settlements or the establishment of *yeshivot* on the West Bank, or marches and demonstrations in favor of settlement, their contact with the Arabs grew and intensified. By and large, it was an antagonistic contact, based on the fact that the Jewish vanguard came into conflict with Arab claims and rejected them.

The religious camp as such is divided on the issue of the future of the territories. Most of its adherents share Begin's view of finding some way to hold on to them, but many of the most orthodox — Agudat Israel, for example — are quite willing to withdraw even from historic holy sites for the sake of real peace. A very small handful of extremists, by no means all religious, would like to see the Arabs expelled from the land. At the same time, the religious mainstream has a hard time accepting the absorption of the mass of Palestinian Arabs as equal citizens, not because these Jews reject civil equality for Arabs — they do not — but because they are concerned about the Jewish character of the state. A large, significant segment of the religious community, particularly from the religious socialist parties, shares Labor's view that since the Palestinian Arabs also have legitimate claims, partition in some form leading to the separation of the two communities is the best way to enable both to maintain their respective national characteristics and personalities. In any case, the original position of the religious camp has collapsed because its members no longer find it possible to ignore the Arabs and still achieve their goals as Jews and Zionists.

Before the Six Day War and After

After Israel's independence was achieved, Labor not only maintained control of the government of the new Jewish state, but its position became the official Israeli position on the Palestinian

73

Arabs. The self-induced mass exodus of Arabs from the territory of the infant state strengthened this policy as a natural one. Had there been a very large Arab minority scattered throughout the country, Israeli Jews might have had to confront the existence of the Palestinian Arabs in a different way. In fact, almost all of the new state was left free of Arabs after 1948, while those Arabs who did not flee were concentrated in the Galilee, particularly in its central and western portions where there were few Jews. Hence a natural geographic separation reinforced other factors making for a separationist solution. Moreover, as the remaining Arabs tended to be rural peasants, there was little economic contact between the two groups.

The Labor-dominated Israeli government pursued a policy of securing group cultural rights for the Arabs by encouraging them to organize municipalities under their own leaders, by providing them with schools in which Arabic was the principal language of instruction, and by extending state support for their religious institutions insofar as they wished to avail themselves of this assistance. Thus, over nearly two decades, a separate Arab society developed within Israel, one that had little contact with the Jews, permitting the latter to virtually ignore the former except in matters of formal government.

At the same time, the Arabs did become citizens of Israel with equivalent civil rights, including the right to vote in Israeli elections. Indeed, they elected a proportionate share of members of the Knesset, a fact guaranteed by the existence of an electoral system based on proportional representation. Even here, the separationist position was maintained through the organization of separate Arab parties, most of which were sponsored by or came under the protection of the mainstream Zionist parties of the Labor camp, in which the Arabs could pursue their own political advantage by linking with the government coalition. The only integrated political parties were Mapam, which until the ninth Knesset always had an Arab Knesset member, and the Communist Party. Because the latter stood outside the Zionist movement, it won the largest share of the Arab vote, and had but few Jewish members, a handful of dedicated Communists who dominated the party leadership. Although the Arabs probably had more in common ideologically with the parties of the civil camp, they saw no advantage to affiliating with what were obviously minority parties unlikely to become part of the governing coalition, much less lead a government. Perhaps surprisingly to those unacquainted with the Israeli scene, the National Religious Party also developed a modest but significant base of support in the Arab sector, in part because of NRP control of the Interior Ministry which is responsible for funding and overseeing local government.

Israelis viewed the Palestinians outside the boundaries of the state as refugees held hostage by the Arab countries in which they found themselves, or as terrorists seeking the destruction of Israel. In the former capacity, Israelis pitied them but believed their condition was perpetuated by an Arab world seeking to foster hatred of Israel. In the latter case, they were simply enemies to be fought with every possible means.

All of this must be perceived in a context in which the Jews, like the rest of the world for that matter, never considered the Palestinians as a separate entity, certainly not within the Arab world. For them, Palestinians were just like all other Arabs who happened to have lived in Palestine. While the more sophisticated Israeli Jews did understand that there were cultural and even linguistic differences among Palestinians, Egyptians, Syrians, Iraqis and others, and while students of the field were aware of the religious sectarianism within Islam, it was an accepted axiom that Arabs were Arabs.

This view was as characteristic of the Arabs as of non-Arabs. Indeed, the only disagreement one heard in the Arab world was about whether the national spirit should be developed in the direction of Pan-Arabism or Pan-Islam. Christian Arabs, including the Palestinians among them, advocated Pan-Arabism and resisted Pan-Islam for obvious reasons.

Elsewhere in this volume, the emergence of a Palestinian identity is discussed at length. Suffice it to say that as long as the Arabs of Palestine were struggling against the Zionists alone, they did not particularly foster a separate Palestinian identity. That identity, to the extent that it exists, was forged in the aftermath of the creation of Israel, principally as the Palestinians' response to their confrontation with their Arab brethren in the Arab states of the

Middle East, as much, if not more than, a result of their confrontation with Israel.

The Palestinians' sense of being outsiders, supported with lip service but rejected in reality by their fellow Arabs, has created what I have termed elsewhere a Palestinian "public," that is to say, a body of people tied together by common intergenerational interests based upon shared externalities and a common vital issue. The final impetus for the emergence of this public came in the aftermath of the Six Day War. The Palestinians, who up to that time had been moving to integrate themselves into Jordan (which, after all, was and is a Palestinian state except for its ruling family), suddenly found themselves divided territorially between an East Bank that remained under Hussein's rule and a West Bank occupied by Israel as a result of a disastrous war. They also confronted an Arab world that, at the very least, was ambivalent toward them.

Given the relatively late emergence of a shared identity among the Palestinians, it is no wonder that Israeli Jews have taken even longer to acknowledge the reality of a separate Palestinian identity. For example, throughout her term as Prime Minister, Golda Meir refused to recognize any Palestinian public, much less a Palestinian people, arguing openly and forcefully against the existence of such a group. During those years, her view was shared by a majority of Israelis. It was not easy to disabuse them of such a view, given the fact that the refugee camps swarmed with non-Palestinians who had acquired refugee identity cards in order to gain the benefits of UN relief efforts, while the terrorist organizations actively recruited non-Palestinians for their missions as readily as they recruited Palestinians.

Many Israelis today are at least grudgingly willing to recognize some sense of "Palestinian-ness" among the Arabs in the territories or those who trace their roots to western Palestine. But most remain quite skeptical of the long-range survival of such an identity. Many view the claim of the Palestinians and other Arabs as a tactical maneuver to evoke world sympathy for yet another Arab state in historic Eretz Israel (there already is Jordan) without any basis in national realities. On the other hand, Palestinian persistence in proclaiming a collective identity has had its effect on Israeli opinion, to the point where even Prime Minister Begin speaks of "Palestinian Arabs." If Israeli Jews do not have a firm "fix" on who is a Palestinian or whether being one is more than a temporary expedient, they are not so different from the Palestinians themselves, except only that the Israelis have a greater interest in moving cautiously toward any recognition of Palestinian identity as well as a greater skepticism about it.

The aftermath of the Six Day War brought an influx of Palestinian Arabs into the Israeli economy and an influx of Israelis, visitors or settlers, into Arab territory. Contacts were established where none had existed before. For Israelis, these contacts were seen as basically non-committal. The Palestinian Arabs were there; they had to live. Therefore, it was reasonable to do business with them and to give them jobs. The territories were there and, since they had strategic, historic and religious value, it was good to settle parts of them where strategic, historic, or religious considerations were involved. By and large, however, the two populations continued to go in their own separate directions.

Since the Israelis did not face up to a final disposition of the territories, they paid relatively little attention to the ultimate relationship that would have to develop between Israeli Jews and Palestinian Arabs, except for those who persisted in their old positions. Thus the Likud, emphasizing that Israel was in the territories to stay, also stressed the necessity of bringing the Palestinian Arabs into the polity as individual citizens. (It should be noted that Begin did not insist on any particular course of action in this regard while he was in the government between 1967 and 1970.) The old-line Labor activists opposed the retention of the densely populated parts of the territories on the ground that the natural increase of the Arab population would drastically dilute, and perhaps even end, the Jewish majority. They also feared that the transfer of most of the less attractive jobs from Jewish to Arab hands would be demoralizing to the Jewish population and a violation of the principles upon which socialist Zionism was built.

For many years, neither of these groups dominated the government, which remained in the hands of "pragmatists" who avoided making strategic decisions, although they pursued practical goals that led to the integration of the territories into the Israeli economic and security systems. The principal Israeli leaders, like those of so much of the rest of the world in the 1960s and 1970s, were ultra-pragmatic in the sense that they avoided actions deliberately directed to the advancement of ideological goals. The result was ad hoc decisions without ever reaching a defined long-range policy, in the hope that such decisions would ultimately lead to conditions in which an appropriate policy could be framed.

Between 1967 and 1973, while Israel had the upper hand in the region, the inhabitants of the administered territories were relatively quiescent, so that the pragmatists' policy continued unchallenged and even seemed to be working. After the Yom Kippur War, it had to change, as did Israeli attitudes towards the Palestinian Arabs who gained new confidence in resisting any extension of the Israeli presence. Moreover, the world began to press Israel to recognize the Palestinians as a people with legitimate national rights.

With its victory in the 1977 elections, the Likud undertook to fulfill its vision that the territories be absorbed into Israel as a matter of historic, military, and religious necessity. As world pressure and local resistance grew, supporters of Likud policy became more desperate to implant a Jewish presence in these territories. At the same time, the Israeli government sought more anxiously a way out of the impasse, as American pressure for an agreement increased. Out of this came the first Israeli recognition that the Palestinian Arabs did have some kind of identity, though there emerged no clear-cut understanding, or willingness to reach an understanding, of precisely what that identity was. As suggested above, there was no reason to expect the Israelis to have a clearer sense of Palestinian identity than the Palestinians themselves. On the other hand, Israel's unwillingness to absorb a population whose hostility was becoming increasingly overt made it impossible simply to reject a separate Palestinian identity in favor of the old Revisionist approach.

The end result is continued murkiness, coupled with a desire not only to have one's cake and eat it too, but to avoid defining the cake. The Labor Party has returned to a partitionist position, to the so-called Jordanian option, but without much conviction, particularly since there has been no acceptable response by Jordan. And even Labor would like to define that option in such a way that Israel retains military control of the territories and Jordan gains only civilian rule. It is assumed that economic integration will continue — a position that certainly does not square with Palestinian

78

demands for self-determination. The Likud remains firmly integrationist, but few within its ranks can have many delusions that the Palestinians are content to be simply individual citizens of a Jewish Israel without expressing any national identity of their own other than their Arabness.

The religious community is divided between those who believe that the preservation of the Jewishness of the state requires repartition and those who believe the achievement of the Jewish national-religious vision demands continued Jewish control of the territories. The resulting views are spread over the whole spectrum of perceptions. They range from the position that the Palestinians, whoever they are, represent a non-Jewish threat to the Jewishness of the state and that therefore their areas should be separated from it, to those who support the notion of civil equality for all as long as the Jews can settle wherever they wish in Eretz Israel, all the way to those few who see the Palestinians as implacable enemies who must be controlled or expelled.

For all the above groups, and for those who have no clear positions on the issue, an Israeli national consensus remains: no separate Palestinian state west of Jordan, no recognition of the Palestine Liberation Organization as the spokesman for the Palestinians whoever they may be, no Israeli withdrawal to the pre-1967 borders, no redivision of Jerusalem, and no substantial return of Arab refugees to Israeli territories.

Notes

1. It should be noted that Hashomer Hatzair, later the Mapam Party, at the extreme left of the Labor Zionist camp, advocated a binational state by the mid-1920s and continued to do so until the 1940s. A major resolution to that effect was formally adopted at the founding conference of the Kibbutz Artzi Hashomer Hatzair in 1927. Mapam has since abandoned that position for a partitionist one but with a confederal option.

2. Allon's original plan was based on the military technology of the Six Day War, which was still a generation behind that of the weaponry used in Vietnam. Moreover, it assumed a clear division of areas of Jewish and Arab settlement in the administered territories. The post-1967 years brought a radical transformation of the military weaponry introduced to the Middle East so that, rather than lagging behind, both sides possessed and used the most advanced weapons systems in the world. New policies had to be designed with that fact in mind. Also, for reasons Allon rejected on a political level but was not entirely out of sympathy with on an emotional one, as the areas of Jewish settlement became increasingly intermixed with those of the Arab population, he recognized that, in practice, those settlements would not be evacuated. Finally, and perhaps most important for him, the integration of the territories and their populations into the Israeli economy, which brought prosperity to both peoples, had to be taken into account. He concluded that the Allon Plan should be implemented with regard to separating Jewish and Arab territories, but that some way should be found to confederate the two entities.

Galia Golan

THE VIEW FROM MOSCOW

Soviet interest in the Middle East in general, and in the Arab-Israeli conflict in particular, has long been determined by global considerations. The Soviet Union supported the founding of the State of Israel as a means of reducing British influence in a region so close to its borders and so vital to the waterways linking West and East. But it did not take long for Moscow to realize that the West could be fully ousted from the area — and Soviet penetration facilitated — by abandoning its early position regarding Israel and by building bridges to the Arab world.

The Soviet Union began to exploit the Arab-Israeli conflict to this end, particularly after Stalin's death in 1953, encouraging Arab states' hostility towards Israel in the hope of rendering them dependent on Soviet military and economic assistance. During the 1960s, the Middle East assumed a higher place on Moscow's list of priorities as a result of a change in Soviet military strategy. Expanding its fleet and conventional military capabilities, as well as seeking a means to counter United States submarine nuclear missile launchers, the Soviet Union inaugurated its Mediterranean Squadron and sought port facilities, and naval and air bases in the eastern Mediterranean. While this effort was part of the broader Soviet-American global strategic competition which was destined to shift further south to the Indian Ocean, it was significant enough to warrant stationing close to 20,000 Soviet military advisers in Egypt and opening several Soviet air and naval facilities there in the late 1960s.

When these benefits were lost in the early 1970s, in the course of the late Egyptian President Anwar Sadat's moves to curtail Soviet influence, Moscow shifted its pursuit of bases and influence to Syria and, less successfully, to Libya. These efforts were a clear indication of how little control Moscow had, in fact, been able to maintain over Egypt, its closest ally in the Middle East. Total dependence on Soviet arms notwithstanding, Egypt could and did shake loose of the Soviet Union virtually overnight. One of the reasons for the rift was Soviet refusal to agree to Sadat's plan for war against Israel in the early 1970s — and therein lay the basic Soviet dilemma with regard to the Arab-Israeli conflict. Desiring to see the conflict perpetuated as a vehicle for their own penetration of the area, the Soviets feared that if it erupted into full-scale war, they would face a confrontation with the United States, in view of the latter's commitment to Israel's security.

The 1973 war — if not the 1967 war — demonstrated just how risky the situation was (including the risk of superpower confrontation) as well as the ability of Moscow's clients to act independently of its wishes.[1] As Arab independence grew with the help of the petrodollar, America's own importance in the region increased at the expense of the Soviet Union's. All these factors led Moscow to seek a way to remain in the Middle East without having to depend on the Arabs and without risking a major conflict in which it, too, would become involved. By seeking to be a partner in a negotiated settlement of the Arab-Israel conflict, Moscow hoped to have its presence in the area internationally recognized and secure, leaving it free to pursue what it now considered a more important objective: its rivalry with the United States in the Persian Gulf and the Indian Ocean. To pressure both Israel and the United States to satisfy this objective, the Soviet Union has deepened its relationship with the more radical Arab states and with the PLO, all of which oppose any settlement with Israel.

This somewhat cynical manipulation, motivated purely by Moscow's interest to limit Western influence, has been typical of its relations with Third World countries and with national liberation movements. When their interest is served by good relations with ruling regimes — even of an anti-Communist "bourgeois" nature — the Soviets will pursue such relations, often at the expense of local Communists or national liberation movements. When its role in the East-West competition is better advanced by supporting a

81

particular national liberation movement, Moscow will do so even if the ideological or socioeconomic credentials of such a movement are far from consistent with its own proletarian credo. To assuage its conscience, Moscow claims that the nationalism of an "oppressed people" — as distinct from that of an "oppressor" — is legitimate, much the way it distinguishes between "just" and "unjust" wars. Similarly, its definition of "people" expands or contracts to fit the movement it wishes to promote or attack. It considers the Palestinians a people, for example, because they have their own land, history, culture and even specific language; but it denies the Jews the same status, claiming they have neither a land nor a specific language — nor a culture. In 1947-48 the Soviets' position had been the exact reverse; at that time, it suited their global interests to support the Jewish national liberation movement against the demands of the Arabs, including the Palestinian Arabs.

Shifts in the Soviet View of the PLO

Soviet involvement in the Palestinian issue has been determined by tactical considerations rather than by any intrinsic interest in the Palestinian problem. When the Palestinian Liberation Organization (PLO) was founded in 1964, the Soviet Union refused to receive its leader, Ahmad Shuqayri, maintaining a decidedly cool, often openly disparaging attitude towards the organization, even in the period immediately following the Six Day War when Shuqayri was replaced by Hamudi. The Soviets did not view the Palestinian movement in terms of a people seeking national liberation or as a central issue in the Arab-Israeli conflict, which they regarded as being waged exclusively by the Arab states and Israel. For them, the Palestinian issue reduced itself to a refugee problem, which was secondary to and dependent on a resolution of Israel's clash with the Arab states.

Only toward the end of the decade did the Soviet attitude change: Yasir Arafat, who had taken over the leadership of the PLO, went on a secret trip to Moscow in 1968 as a member of an Egyptian delegation. By now, the Soviets had begun to recognize the Palestinians as a people, occasionally even referring to their cause as a movement for national liberation. This they followed with open political support, indirect arms deliveries and facilities for military training, and by extending a warm welcome to Arafat, who headed a PLO delegation to Moscow in 1970 — albeit at a non-governmental, non-party level. The Soviets also set up their own Palestinian organization, al-Ansar, within the PLO, to provide them with a direct line of information and influence. The organization died a natural death in 1972 for lack of Palestinian support. Soviet aid became much more open and significant in 1972, when an agreement was signed with Arafat in Moscow for direct supplies of Soviet arms and equipment; these indeed began to arrive in Damascus in the fall.

The shift in Soviet attitude may have been connected with the increase in publicity given to the PLO and the effectiveness of its terrorist operations, or due to Soviet competition with the Chinese (who had been aiding the PLO from the start). But the main reason for Moscow's change of heart was tactically dictated by regional interests: Soviet support of the PLO came only after Egypt, Moscow's largest and most powerful client in the region, openly adopted the PLO, and when the Arab states began to use the Palestinian issue as a major feature of their own tactics. Still, Moscow continued to define the Arab-Israeli conflict as one between states in the Middle East. As late as December 1973, in his speech to the Geneva Peace Conference, Soviet Foreign Minister Andrei Gromyko ranked the Palestinian issue behind what he called the "key problems": the lands occupied by Israel in 1967.

Only in late 1973, indeed officially and publicly only in the fall of 1974, did the Soviet Union abandon its explicit opposition to the idea of a Palestinian state. The reasons it had been hesitating for so long were probably threefold: misgivings about the complications and difficulties which would arise from the demand for statehood; a relatively low opinion of the PLO as an organization sufficiently strong or unified to warrant Soviet commitment; and the split within the PLO itself over the problems connected with declaring a state (e.g., the need to specify the borders of such a state). A change in this last factor may have accounted for the shift in the Soviet position. While the Soviets were still unwilling to speak directly of a state (they merely used the term "national rights"), probably because the PLO itself still refrained from doing so publicly, some groups within the PLO, including to some degree the dominant Fatah, were willing to entertain the idea of a mini-state on the West Bank and Gaza, at least as a "first step."

The reasons for the Soviet shift may, however, reflect broader considerations. One of Moscow's tactics after the Yom Kippur War was to champion the demands of the more radical Arab states. In this way it could present itself to the Arabs as the only superpower interested in a comprehensive settlement rather than in the partial agreements offered by the United States, while persuading the Americans and the Israelis that Moscow alone could control the war option, moderate the radicals or even bring them to the negotiating table. Increasing its support of the PLO and the idea of a Palestinian state may have been part of this tactic. It is also possible that the Soviets sought an additional option for taking part in the negotiations following the Yom Kippur War. They were primarily concerned with the growing influence of the United States in the region and with the emerging American-Egyptian relationship. They were anxious to participate in whatever talks might occur between Jordan and Israel, both of which had been exclusively American clients until then.

In the fall of 1974, Soviet leadership finally openly advocated the creation of a Palestinian state, incorporating this demand into the standard Soviet formula for a Middle East settlement. This step, coming as it did just before the Rabat conference of Arab heads of state, can be explained by a variety of reasons. The Soviets were probably aware that the Arab leaders were planning to pass a resolution in favor of a Palestinian state on the West Bank and Gaza, and armed with this prior knowledge, could formulate their own declarations in such a way as to make them acceptable to the Arabs. In this same context, however, was Soviet concern over the pro-American stance that Egypt would be advocating in Rabat and, specifically, the very real possibility of continued American progress in the wake of the two disengagement agreements negotiated earlier that year, and the U.S. efforts to open talks for a second Egyptian-Israeli agreement and/or a Jordanian-Israeli disengagement agreement. Such "step-ups" in Soviet support, in response to American achievements, would often occur on later occasions as well, as global and regional considerations became combined in determining the Soviet attitude towards the Palestinians.

As the United States became more and more successful in its involvement in the Middle East, the Soviet commitment to the idea of a Palestinian state became stronger. But the component features of such a state — its location and borders, its relationship with Jordan, the problem of the refugees and the status of Jerusalem — were much less clear and apparently subject to some debate. As a superpower interested in expanding its influence without precipitating a direct confrontation with the United States, the Soviet Union has sought to impose on the PLO what it calls a "realistic" position regarding the details of a Palestinian state. Thus the Soviets even argued with the PLO, particularly with its more radical members, against the idea of supplanting Israel with a Palestinian state. In fact, Moscow repeatedly raised the ire even of its closest allies in the PLO when it urged them to accept a resolution providing for mutual Israeli-PLO recognition. Soviet pressures in this direction were dropped only in 1979, when the United States took up the idea and tried itself to gain a similar type of agreement from the PLO.

The Soviet Position on Israel

The Soviet position on Israel's right to exist has, in fact, been consistent even to the degree of almost wholly ignoring the PLO idea of a democratic secular state in Palestine. This is not to say that Moscow has become pro-Zionist or abandoned its opposition to Zionism as a "bourgeois, racist ideology," harmful to the "real interests of the Israeli nation," as they put it. In their effort arbitrarily to separate the State of Israel and the ideology upon which it is based, the Soviets often reject the existence of a Jewish people, explaining instead that what is being formed in Israel is an Israeli or Hebrew nation. According to this line of thinking, Zionism might disappear if peace were achieved with the Arabs, but not the State of Israel. By the same token, it is not very likely that the Soviets' support for the principle of Israel's right to exist stems from altruism. In their arguments with Palestinians and others, they have explained what is probably the genuine reason for their position: realism. It is simply unrealistic to call for the destruction of Israel, or expect that this would be politically or militarily feasible, without causing a world war. If the constellation of forces in the world were different, if America were to abandon its commitment to Israel, if the European nations were to withdraw their recognition, the Soviet position might well be different. But even the Soviets contend that a historical fact exists and that a realistic position must be adopted in view of present circumstances.

Yet, two issues connected with the idea of a Palestinian state could, by implication, spell the end of the Israeli state: the idea of a return to the Partition Plan of 1947, and the demand for the repatriation of the Arab refugees. Officially, the Soviet Union has never recognized any borders for Israel but those of 1947, and to this day Soviet maps show these partition lines, the armistice lines of 1949 and the cease-fire lines of 1967. However, since 1968 in negotiations with the United States, and publicly since 1970, Moscow has been referring to the lines of June 4, 1967, which preceded the eruption of the Six Day War (which correspond to the 1949 Armistice Demarcation Lines),as the legitimate borders of the State of Israel, specifying that a Palestinian state must be limited to the West Bank and Gaza. The Soviets even argue that Israel has an opportunity to obtain international recognition of these borders, as distinct from those of the Partition Plan.

This position was expressed by Soviet Foreign Minister Gromyko in his opening speech to the Geneva Peace Conference in 1973 and is embodied in the Soviets' standard three-clause formula for a settlement which calls for what Moscow terms "organically interlinked" steps: Israeli withdrawal from the territories occupied in 1967; the creation of a Palestinian state; and international guarantees for the independence, territorial integrity and security of all states in the area, including Israel. The Soviets here specifically stated and increasingly emphasized that the location for a Palestinian state must be the West Bank and Gaza. Such insistence has become more frequent in response to Israel's autonomy plan for what Moscow claims are precisely those territories which should constitute the Palestinian state. Following the PLO plan sent to President Carter through the Saudis in May 1977, which called for East Jerusalem as the capital of a Palestinian state, and especially after Sadat's visit, the Soviets also began to include Jerusalem in the new state. Usually referring to *East* Jerusalem, they rarely if ever mentioned the plan of 1947 for the internationalization of the city; they have alleged on occasion that even West Jerusalem is not legally Israel's capital.

The Soviets have posited the borders existing immediately before the Six Day War as the dividing line between Israel and the Palestinian state. They have said so in their conversations — and their arguments — with the Palestinians themselves, as well as with such rejectionist states as Libya and Iraq. It is also the position of the Soviet-dominated Israel Communist Party (Rakah), as opposed to that of the nationalist Israeli Arab group called Sons of the Village. Moscow has tried to present this position as "realistically" accepted by the PLO, often quoting statements by Naif Hawatmeh and Faruq Qaddoumi on this issue. The Soviets carefully refrain from citing these leaders when they say that such a state on the West Bank and Gaza is only a first step in the eventual creation of a Palestinian state in all of Palestine.

On the other hand, Soviet references to the UN Partition Plan of 1947 can still be heard whenever it is evoked as a legitimization of the Palestinian demand for a state. For the most part, Soviet pronouncements go on to specify the site of the Palestinian state, thereby indicating that they are *not* advocating the return of Israel to the 1947 borders. But occasionally they add a commentary which is vague even to the point of implying that the lines of 1967 might be only a first step. This ambiguity suggests that the whole border issue is employed tactically — in a carrot-and-stick approach — towards both Israel and the PLO. Both public and private Soviet references to the borders of June 4, 1967, have been particularly in evidence when there appear to be good chances for setting up multilateral negotiations that include the Soviet Union, i.e., when the Soviets are particularly interested in convincing Israel that Moscow would be a reasonable partner in the negotiations. That the Soviet preference for the borders of June 4, 1967, is more than tactical, however, is suggested by the fact that Moscow has pursued this line even when acknowledging opposition to it by Palestinians and other Arabs, and even in private discussion with these parties. As with the existence of Israel, so too with regard to the borders of 1967 versus those of 1947, the Soviet position is declaredly and probably genuinely based on "realism." Israel has existed within the borders of June 4, 1967, since 1949; for all intents and purposes they have been recognized at least as *de facto* borders, and any attempt to reduce the Jewish State to the truncated model advocated by the Partition Plan would amount to an effort to destroy Israel.

Similarly the issue of the return of the refugees might prove contradictory to the Soviet position regarding Israel's existence. In 1948, the Soviet Union officially supported Resolution 194 of the UN General Assembly as well as subsequent resolutions which called for the return of the Palestinian refugees or for compensation, but it rarely mentioned the issue as such, referring more generally to a "just solution" of the problem, according to the wording of Security Council Resolution 242 of November 22, 1967. While supporting the various resolutions of the UN General Assembly which defined the issue more specifically, Moscow itself suddenly began, in the summer of 1977, to include in its formula for a settlement the demand for the refugees' right to return — at least as reported in the press and in joint communiqués with Arab delegations. Coming as it did shortly after President Carter's speech in Clinton, Massachusetts, in which he recognized the Palestinians' right to a "homeland," this step-up in the Soviets' support for the PLO may have been an attempt to outbid Washington. Certainly their propaganda reflected their sensitivity to the very real possibility that the PLO might turn toward America. The plan the PLO sent to the U.S. in May 1977 specified the refugee issue. The PLO also pressed Egypt to add this point to Cairo's "working paper" in August 1977. And it is likely that the PLO's own insistence at this time may have been a response to U.S. comments that large-scale return of refugees was to be ruled out.

The Soviets claim that the return of the refugees need not infringe upon Israel's rights, but just what rights they mean is placed in doubt by such statements as one made by Moscow to the effect that such a return could threaten "only the rule of clerical Zionist circles in Israel, but not the existence of the State of Israel." A difference between the interpretation of the PLO and that of the Soviets may be indicated, however, by a certain ambiguity in Soviet formulations regarding the territory to which the refugees are to return. The PLO speaks of their "original homes and properties" or "hearths," and occasionally the Soviets agree to this wording in joint communiqués with visiting Arabs. But a number of Soviet commentaries and even official statements have either implied or directly stated that the refugee problem would be solved by the creation of a Palestinian state on the West Bank and Gaza, the "return" being to this area rather than to Israel proper. The official Soviet position is probably intentionally ambiguous. Aside from occasional pressure from the PLO or the need, tactically, to respond to American statements, the Soviets have probably preferred to avoid irritating Israel on this delicate issue or confronting the problem head-on before the time for explicit formulations is clearly imminent.

The Soviet Attitude to Jordan

On the subject of a Palestinian state's eastern border, or on the relations of such a state to Jordan, the Soviets are almost totally silent. By implication, of course, advocating a state limited to the territories occupied by Israel in 1967 delineates the eastern border as well. In theory, at least, this need not rule out a federal Palestinian-Jordanian solution, and at various times over the past years the Soviets have shown signs of supporting such an idea. They have probably sought to maintain as many options open as possible, including a positive relationship with King Hussein, despite the opposition of many elements in the PLO and even of the Jordanian Communists. This is part of the Soviets' traditional preference for relations with established states and stable regimes, often at the expense of local Communists or national liberation movements.

But even while urging PLO-Jordanian cooperation, by 1978 the Soviets did come out explicitly against the idea of confederation or federation by denying any Jordanian claim to the West Bank. This position emerged in response to Egyptian proposals for links between a Palestinian state and Jordan, and later, to confederation ideas brought up by the United States and Israel. In both cases, Moscow's opposition to these ideas not only mirrored that of the PLO, but reflected its own policy. After Sadat's visit to Jerusalem in 1977, the Soviets began to emphasize the Palestinians' claim to the West Bank — as distinct from Jordan's — without, however, criticizing Hussein himself. In fact, this apparently negative attitude towards Jordan (the Soviets pointed out that hardly any countries had ever recognized Jordan's annexation of the West Bank in 1950) was initially accompanied by Soviet talks with Crown Prince Hassan, in order to keep Jordan from joining the Egyptian-American peace effort.

This dual approach was indicative of a certain contradiction in Moscow's position, which was to become all the more apparent in the wake of the Egyptian-Israeli peace treaty. Until the Camp David Accords, it had continued to grant to Amman the status of partner in any proposed negotiations for settling the Arab-Israeli conflict. As noted, only in response to Egyptian initiatives did the Soviets explicitly begin to deny Jordan the right to negotiate the fate of the West Bank, and only in November 1978, in reaction to Camp David and the Israeli autonomy plan for the West Bank and Gaza, did the Soviets finally grant the PLO official status as the "sole legitimate representative of the Palestinian people," reasoning that neither Jordan nor "local Quislings" could take the place of the PLO in determining the future of the West Bank. Having said this, and actively encouraging a policy of non-cooperation by both Jordan and the Palestinians regarding the autonomy plan (primarily as a means to foil the American-sponsored peace effort), the Soviets are nevertheless trying to keep certain avenues open for themselves within the new context. Thus they have maintained contacts with King Hussein while simultaneously collaborating on the West Bank with anti-Jordanian rejectionist elements, even to the point of criticizing PLO-Jordanian rapprochement.

Relations With Dissident Factions in the PLO

The lack of unity within the PLO itself has greatly hampered Soviet activity. Moscow's influence is further limited by the fact that many, if not all, of the contending groups that make up the PLO are linked to and supported by various Arab states, whereas the PLO as a whole is financially dependent on Saudi Arabia. Of these groups, Moscow supports Fatah, despite this organization's expressly non-ideological nature and the presence of right-wing Muslim traditionalists in its midst. Although the Soviets are critical of this situation and have sought to impose a more ideological approach, they see some positive value in Fatah's nationalist position, as a counterbalance to the extremist ideologies of some of the rejectionist groups and countries. However, the fact that Fatah is by far the largest and still the dominant group in the PLO is undoubtedly the major reason for Moscow's support.

Ideologically the Soviets are much more comfortable with Naif Hawatmeh, leader of the Popular Democratic Front for the Liberation of Palestine (PDFLP). While they deem him too extremist at times, Hawatmeh is much less radical, closer to the Soviet line than the other Marxist group led by George Habash. For this reason Hawatmeh has been cultivated by the Soviet Union, invited to Moscow independently of the PLO, and often singled out as a moderate. Indeed, according to reports in the Arab world, he has even served as mediator on behalf of the Soviets in such areas as Eritrea. All in all, however, the PDFLP is an extremely small, relatively uninfluential group within the PLO, promising little in the way of future power for the Soviets.

The other Marxist in the PLO, George Habash, the leader of the Popular Front for the Liberation of Palestine (PFLP), has had very poor relations with Moscow. The Soviets have engaged in open polemics with him over almost every conceivable issue: the idea of a mini-state on the West Bank and Gaza, the existence of Israel, Resolution 242, the very notion of negotiating with Israel, cooperation with King Hussein, the use of terror, immigration of Soviet Jews to Israel, and other issues. The Soviets have openly denounced Habash as too extremist and have specifically rejected his (and Hawatmeh's) use of terror. While the Soviets themselves train Palestinians in guerrilla warfare, they would rather that this method be subordinated to political measures and limited to sabotage or resistance, preferably in the territories occupied by Israel. International terror is not advocated, ostensibly because Moscow considers it counterproductive, possibly because the Soviets themselves are vulnerable to and have been victims of hijackings. Nevertheless, the KGB is actively involved, *sub rosa*, in the training of subversive elements all over the world, which makes the Soviet connection with international terrorism more than hypothetical, especially in view of the fact that the Soviet-trained Palestinians are themselves suppliers and advisors to numerous terrorist organizations such as the Red Brigades, the Japanese Red Army and the Turkish People's Liberation Army. The Soviets have openly — and privately — criticized Habash on this issue, and Habash in turn has criticized the Soviets for, among other things, their rejection of terrorism.

Despite their distate for Habash, the Soviets have maintained contact with him through their allies in Eastern Europe and China. A brief rapprochement between Moscow and Habash even took place during the Lebanese civil war (when Arafat made an alliance with him), and again more recently as part of the coalition formed in opposition to the Egyptian-Israeli peace treaty. Habash visited the USSR in November 1978, and the Soviet media clearly changed their tone towards him, particularly after he, unlike Arafat, expressed unreserved support for the invasion of Afghanistan.

This situation reflects the overall Soviet position on the rejectionists within the PLO, i.e., opposing their more radical, sometimes pro-Chinese, extremist ideas and methods, while nonetheless seeking to maintain a relationship with them for the purpose of gaining influence over them, possibly tempering them or, at the very least, exploiting the specific congruence of interests that has developed in response to the Egyptian-Israeli treaty. The Soviets do seem to be interested in the Palestinian rejectionists at present as the group which might prevent the less ideological Arafat from turning towards the Americans. Indeed, on the West Bank, where local rejectionists have been gaining strength against the less radical pro-Fatah groups currently aligned with Jordan, the Soviets find themselves on the rejectionists' side. But the rejectionists' overall lack of unity and strength within the PLO, their attachment to outside Arab governments, particularly Iraq and Libya, and their extremist bellicose views prevent them from being a satisfying partner for Moscow's efforts.

Other Groups

Independently of their own preferences or problems among the Palestinian factions, the Soviets developed their own organization, the Palestine National Front (PNF). The creation of this group by the Jordanian Communist Party in 1973 may in fact have been evidence of Soviet preparations for the eventuality of a Palestinian state. The PNF was said to be a non-party, all-embracing political organization for the West Bank and Gaza. In this sense it was similar to the classical "Fronts" set up by the Communists in occupied Europe during World War II, Communist-dominated coalitions which eventually took over the countries of Eastern Europe. The PNF, as a member of the PLO which included PLO forces, was said to be the nucleus of the future Palestinian government in the West Bank and Gaza in which the Communists admittedly would play an active but not exclusive role. Most likely Moscow intended it to dominate the PLO from within by becoming the leading comprehensive force on the West Bank. Although quite successful in the municipal elections held on the West Bank in 1976, the PNF remained extremely weak, also severely crippled by Israeli deportations of many of its activists. The PNF would appear to have been supplanted *de facto* by the National Guidance Committees created after the Camp David Accords. Although the Communists were among those who set them up, they rapidly lost to the local rejectionists whatever influence they had intended to have there.

As Soviet support grew for the idea of a Palestinian state, Moscow not only stressed the PNF as the nucleus and framework for an eventual Palestinian government, but also made greater use of local Communists, particularly the Jordanian Communist Party (which is illegal in Jordan). In 1974 this party converted its West Bank branch into the Palestinian Communist Organization (PCO) with an estimated membership of 100 persons; and in 1982 the PCO became an independent Palestinian Communist Party. The Communists have been particularly active in recruitment and propaganda, suggesting a dual Soviet purpose: to be prepared, organizationally as well as politically, for the possibility of autonomy, and to insure a more "progressive" ideological line to counter American advances, or Saudi influence, or even Fatah's non-ideological fare. The work has been complicated of late because of local rejectionist opposition to the mainstream PLO policy of cooperation with Jordan, including pro-Jordanian and even traditional Muslim forces on the West Bank. This cooperation, the result of PLO-Jordanian rapprochement, is viewed with suspicion by Moscow, not only because it tends to exclude the local

Communists but also because it raises the specter of a pro-Western, pro-American orientation within the PLO.

Indeed, a decided strain has developed in Soviet-PLO relations over the past year because of a number of factors. Moscow has been worried about PLO efforts to open a dialogue with the United States and Europe, and to maintain contacts with Egypt, whereas the PLO has been unhappy with Soviet failure to supply the type of arms it wants for fighting in southern Lebanon. (In fact, though the Soviets supported the PLO against Syria in the Lebanese civil war during 1975-76, the latter complained even then that Soviet aid was neither sufficient nor direct.) Apparently Moscow is also concerned about Arafat's interest in Islamic renaissance since this interest significantly tempered the support Moscow was able to obtain from him on the Afghanistan issue. Formally the PLO fell in line with pro-Soviet states on this matter, but enthusiastic support could be obtained only from Habash and Hawatmeh.

Future Problems

Both the lack of unity within the PLO and the problems Moscow has with the Palestinians provide some indication of the relationship the Soviet Union might have with a future Palestinian state. While Soviet support for the PLO and Palestinian statehood has been primarily of a tactical nature — a function of Moscow's relations with the Arab countries and of its competition with the United States — it is also intended to secure a viable Soviet foothold in the state which might emerge. While Moscow can certainly be expected to pursue this objective, there are some questions regarding the price it might have to pay for success.

There is no guarantee that a Palestinian state would be any more certain or stable a Soviet ally than the PLO as a national liberation movement is today. Neither the domestic nor foreign policy orientation of such a state can be entirely clear-cut because of the various and even conflicting ideologies or tendencies within the Palestinian movement: "bourgeois," Muslim conservative, radical Marxist, pro-Chinese, pro-Egyptian, pro-Jordanian (or at least not anti-Jordanian), and even pro-American. Even assuming that the new state would opt for what the Soviets call a non-capitalist path of development oriented towards the Soviet-led socialist camp, the problem of control would still remain. In pursuit of this control, the Soviets would have to cope with the heavy burden of insuring the state's economic viability and providing for its defense. These tasks are both costly and risky; as past Soviet relations with Third World states prove, they do not guarantee control. As in other Soviet patron-client relationships, the American option for economic assistance would be a persistent threat.

Moreover, the Soviets could not count on financial benefit from supplying the Palestinian state with arms if the Arab countries were unwilling to pay the bills. If a war broke out with Israel, the Soviet Union would face many of the same problems it has in the past with regard to Egypt and Syria. The classic dilemma would return: supplying arms in order to gain influence but thereby augmenting the risk of war and possible Arab (Palestinian) defeat, the ensuing blow to Soviet prestige, the need for Soviet intervention, possible escalation, the danger of superpower confrontation — or failure to make any inroads or gain any influence at all. Even if the new state pursued a moderate course, there would be a problem over the continued operations of dissident Palestinian groups which, in turn, would incur the threat of Israeli reprisal, perhaps lead to war or, at the very least, create troublesome instability for the Moscow-backed regime.

The Palestinian problem is not a priority matter for the Soviet Union in the Middle East. Used tactically to undermine the Americans and curry favor with the radical Arab regimes, it has never directly affected Soviet relations with the Persian Gulf states — which today assume a much higher priority in Soviet policy-making than the rest of the Middle East. In fact, there is no guarantee that a Palestinian state will not actually complicate Soviet-Saudi or Soviet-Khomeini relations in the event that the conservative Muslim influence of Saudi Arabia or Iran leads to conflict with Moscow over the nature of a local Palestinian regime or its independence.

The Soviets appear to be well aware of the uncertainty and instability likely to characterize their relationship with a Palestinian state. They aspire to build the kind of relationship they have with Syria and South Yemen, or the one with Libya, if necessary. But they are also preparing other options in case the relationship becomes like the one with Iraq or — worst of all from Moscow's point of view — turns sour like the Soviet-Egyptian alliance.

Moscow appears to be willing to run the risks and pay the costs, much as it does today with regard to Syria, in exchange for a presence in the area. It seeks to exploit the Palestinian issue as it suits its interests, apparently confident that a Palestinian state almost anywhere on the scale of friendship with the Soviet Union — whether along the Syrian or the Libyan model — will, on balance, be an asset in its competition with the United States.

Note

1. For details of the Egyptian-Soviet relationship before and during the Yom Kippur War, see the author's *Yom Kippur and After: The Soviet Union and the Middle East Crisis* (Cambridge: Cambridge University Press, 1977).

Rita E. Hauser

IMPLICATIONS FOR
UNITED STATES POLICY

As the essays in this volume demonstrate, the Palestinian issue has moved from the realm of the humanitarian problems of displaced refugees to a classic political dilemma in which a defined group of people with a group self-identity seeks a political expression of that identity in statehood. Resolution 242 of the UN Security Council, adopted unanimously after the Six Day War, speaks of "achieving a just settlement of the refugee problem" and was intended to cover both Arab and Jewish refugee claims to either repatriation or resettlement and compensation.

UN Resolutions and Other Early Agreements

Resolution 242 makes no direct reference to a Palestinian people. Lord Caradon, the British delegate who drafted the final text, has explained that the omission was deliberate, for none of the Arab states at the time asked for a separate Palestinian state, but demanded instead that the territories occupied by Israel in the war be returned respectively to Egypt, Syria and Jordan. The resolution, which was based on the peace initiative of President Lyndon B. Johnson and U.S. Ambassador Arthur J. Goldberg, inextricably linked the implementation of the demand on Israel to withdraw its "armed forces from territories occupied in the recent conflict" to Arab readiness formally to end their war against Israel.[1] Under Security Council Resolution 338, unanimously adopted after the 1973 Yom Kippur War, it was decided that the concerned parties should immediately begin negotiations toward a just and durable peace based on "implementation of Resolution 242 (1967) in all of its parts."

97

In contrast to the Security Council, which saw the refugee issue as only one component in Arab-Israel peace negotiations, the UN General Assembly has focused on "the inalienable rights of the people of Palestine." This drive culminated in November 1974 in the Assembly's adoption of Resolution 3236, which recognized that "the Palestinian people is entitled to self-determination" and affirmed the right to "national independence and sovereignty" of the "Palestinian people in Palestine." Among the "inalienable rights" affirmed by the Assembly was the Palestinians' "right to return to their homes and property," and the resolution unqualifiedly called for their return.

Resolution 3236 asserted that the Palestine Liberation Organization is the representative of the Palestinians. (A companion resolution [3237] accorded the PLO official observer status at the UN.) In the Third World, Soviet and Islamic-dominated Assembly, it was approved by a vote of 89 to 8, with most of the European and Latin American states abstaining. The United States strongly opposed it on the ground that it was a one-sided endorsement of the Palestinian claims, and included no reference either to Security Council Resolution 242 nor an acknowledgment of the requirement that the Palestinians also take into account Israel's right, as a UN member, to a secure existence.

Although the Assembly resolution and its specifications are only non-binding recommendations, the basic principle of recognition that the Palestinians were a people in search of a defined homeland was widely endorsed in subsequent years by most of the nations of the world, including West European countries. The Venice Declaration of the European Economic Community in 1980 supported the idea of Palestinian self-determination, but linked it to acceptance of Israel's "right of existence and to security," and to a renunciation of violence by all sides. The EEC also said that the Palestinians and the PLO should be "associated" with the peace negotiations. Many nations have accepted quasi-state visits from Yasir Arafat, the PLO leader, and allowed the PLO to open offices within their territory. While refusing to grant the PLO official status, United States policy towards the Palestinian issue has evolved in the direction of acknowledgment of a political movement. After many years of limiting itself to legitimate "concerns" of the refugees, the U.S. spoke, in the 1977 joint Soviet-U.S. communiqué, of the "legitimate interests" of the Palestinians; and the Camp David Accords of September 1978 call for recognition of the "legitimate rights of the Palestinian people and their just requirements," and invite them to "participate in the determination of their own future."

False Assumptions

Although the United States has not openly endorsed self-determination as a political process that will lead eventually to full Palestinian statehood, there is little doubt that official Washington, particularly in the aftermath of the Yom Kippur War, concluded that the Palestinian issue was crucial to the achievement of a comprehensive Arab-Israel peace and to the promotion of Middle East stability in general.

Candidate Jimmy Carter spoke in 1976 of a "homeland" for the Palestinian refugees, and in 1977 repeated this idea as one of three crucial elements of a lasting settlement; the other two were negotiation of recognized borders and defense arrangements, and the establishment of peace and normal relations between the Arab states and Israel.

The more conservative Arab states, such as Saudi Arabia and Jordan, publicly insist on a resolution of the Palestinian question as essential to stable and productive relations with the United States, and the rejectionist states obviously focus on the unresolved Palestinian problem as the reason for their unremitting antagonism against Israel. The fact that these Arab countries have continually betrayed the Palestinians, as the preceding essays show, does not moderate to any extent their demand that the issue be resolved. The so-called moderates call on the United States to press Israel to withdraw to pre-1967 lines and accept a Palestinian state on the West Bank and in Gaza. But that does not satisfy the "rejectionist" Arab states and the official demands of the PLO; as their vehement opposition to the Fahd plan has demonstrated, they are not prepared for even a tacit, ambiguously worded acknowledgment of Israel's existence. The stumbling block for the United States has been and remains the PLO. Moving toward greater recognition of, and dealing with, the PLO has often been advocated as a means to advance U.S. interests; but those who make this case base it on several assumptions that are open to most serious challenge.

The first assumption is that the PLO is fundamentally moderate, and that only U.S. support for Israel keeps it from becoming, eventually, a force whose interests can be made sufficiently compatible with those of the U.S. This is to deny what the PLO says about itself and its goals with regard to Israel. And the world has paid dearly, in the past, for failing to take seriously what political leaders and groups clearly state to be their aims.

A similar assumption is that if the Palestinian issue is settled, Saudi Arabia, which is emerging more and more as a linchpin in American strategy, will be able to act openly as an American ally in ways it does not do now. Leaving aside whether Saudi Arabia can in fact be a linchpin of American strategy — an issue worthy of discussion by itself — this highly questionable assumption means, again, not believing either the Saudis' historical record in advancing their own interests, or what they are clearly indicating: They do not wish to be too closely tied to the U.S. lest they arouse Soviet ire or inflame hostile Arab elements.

There is, increasingly, another element that needs clarification: to what extent support for the Palestinians today in order to satisfy the Saudis arises not out of any true evaluation of U.S. interests, but simply because there are profits to be made from export sales to the Saudis and other oil-rich nations. This latter consideration is indeed a significant factor in the forging of American policy today.

Finally, the PLO is both a force for terrorism and a Soviet ally. It has achieved a world position through these two roles. As an umbrella organization, the PLO, and especially its more radical member groups, have joined regularly with other states — for example, Libya, Marxist Southern Yemen, Cuba — similarly opposed to fundamental U.S. interests.

Thus, from a strictly American perspective, there are many troubling questions to be resolved before any movement toward the PLO can be considered. Most important is the fact that U.S. interests anywhere in the world are best served when democratic nations and forces are sustained and supported. However, because it is so often forgotten or ignored, the obvious apparently needs repeating: The one democratic country in the Middle East is Israel.

100

Advancing the cause of those who threaten Israel does a disservice to basic American interests.

The Israel-U.S. Agreement on a Geneva Conference and the PLO

One must also remember the background against which the current position on the PLO emerged. Disengagement agreements were concluded between Egypt and Israel and between Syria and Israel in 1974; and on September 1, 1975, a second disengagement agreement was reached between Egypt and Israel under the active diplomatic prodding of Secretary of State Henry Kissinger.

Deeply concerned that the PLO's diplomatic victory in the General Assembly in November 1974 would soon be translated into concrete acts, the Israelis asked for and got reassurances — in Memoranda of Agreement between the then Secretary of State Kissinger and Israeli Foreign Minister Yigal Allon — concerning Security Council Resolution 242 and the PLO.

The United States said it would oppose and, if necessary, veto "any initiative in the Security Council to alter adversely the terms of reference of the Geneva Peace Conference or to change Resolutions 242 and 338 in ways which are incompatible with their original purpose." At the same time, the U.S. also promised to "seek to insure that the role of the co-sponsors" would be consistent with the U.S.-Israeli understanding before the first Geneva Conference in December 1973, which had been designed to prevent the Russians or the Americans from imposing their own terms on the Israelis.

An issue of grave Israeli concern was the growing Arab, Soviet and general international pressure to have the Palestinians — with the PLO as their representatives — considered a separate party to a reconvened Geneva Conference. Some prominent "Palestinians" had, in fact, attended the first Geneva Conference, but they were Palestinian Arabs in the Jordanian delegation (and, indeed, constituted its majority). Kissinger pledged to Allon that the United States policy not to recognize or negotiate with the PLO would continue as long as it "does not recognize Israel's right to exist and does not accept Security Council Resolutions 242 and 338."

Kissinger also reconfirmed the acceptance of Israel's right to veto PLO participation, which Israel had made a condition for its own participation in December 1973. "It is understood," the pertinent paragraph read, "that the participation at a subsequent phase of the conference of any possible additional state, group or organization will require the agreement of all the initial participants." These commitments were reaffirmed by President Carter at Camp David, and again when the Egyptian-Israeli Peace Treaty was signed.

Israel has clung to these commitments, insisting on America's faithful adherence to them as well, and has successfully precluded any direct, overt contacts between the United States and the PLO in the intervening years. The dismissal of UN Ambassador Andrew Young stemmed, in part, from his "unauthorized" contacts with PLO representatives.

Yet, as has been widely suggested, it seems that there have been informal U.S. contacts with the PLO. A strong line of American opinion has emerged, in which influential elements in Washington concur, that it is folly not to talk to the PLO, lest we have no leverage with their leaders at all. There were hints from the Carter Administration implying that such direct contacts would have taken place if he had been reelected in 1980. Nor should it be forgotten that the late Moshe Dayan, then Israeli Foreign Minister, agreed to Palestinian participation in the proposed reconvened Geneva Conference as part of Jordan's delegation. Whether such participants could have had PLO connections was never fully clarified. Moreover, two former Presidents, Carter and Gerald R. Ford, stated to the press on their way home from President Sadat's funeral that the United States would eventually have to communicate with the PLO. Former President Richard M. Nixon has also supported this conclusion.

All stressed, however, that a major stumbling block was the PLO's refusal to recognize Israel or allow other Palestinians to join the negotiations. Carter noted that "the greatest thing the Palestinians could do for themselves is for the Palestinian mayors to say, 'We'll negotiate even this limited self-government or full autonomy.' And then consolidate their position, run their own schools, run their own water supplies, run their own police force, build their own roads and so forth."

The Palestinians did not have to be represented by "Arafat or the highly publicized leaders of the PLO," Carter added. "It can be responsible business and other leaders." Elaborating on this point, Ford noted that "the Palestinian world encompasses a wide variety of very diverse groups, and although Mr. Arafat representing the PLO today is the most visible leader, I am sure in this huge number of people who are of Palestinian origin, there may well be other leaders that in time, either in conjunction with Arafat or independently, will have an opportunity to represent them in these eventual negotiations that have to take place."

Failure to reconvene the Geneva Conference in 1977, President Carter's blunder in prematurely inviting the Soviets back into the process, and inability to reduce Syria's hostility to peace-making, all culminated in Anwar Sadat's historic breakthrough and its result at Camp David: a peace between Egypt and Israel which left the vexing Palestinian issues to be negotiated later on the basis of "full autonomy" for the Palestinians in the West Bank (Judea and Samaria) and the Gaza District. The ultimate disposition of the conflicting territorial claims was to be settled in negotiations among Israel, Egypt, Jordan and the Palestinians that would start in the latter part of a five-year transition period.

Since neither Jordan nor the Palestinians have participated in the desultory, often-adjourned autonomy talks, not much has come of them to date. Although President Carter assigned two high-level special negotiators — Robert Strauss and Sol Linowitz — the United States has been unable to bridge the major differences which still prevail toward the creation of a self-governing authority in the West Bank.

Candidate Ronald Reagan took a very tough line on the PLO, branding its members terrorists and outlaws. However, no sooner had he been sworn in as President than he modified his official line to mean that only some elements of the PLO, not all, fit that description, which seems to leave the door open to negotiating with, or at least speaking to, some PLO representatives. In the post-Camp David atmosphere, the Reagan approach was to move the Palestinian problem to a back burner while, in response to the emerging threats to U.S. interests from the Soviet invasion of Afghanistan, the Iran-Iraq war, and the turmoil in Iran, he vigorously pursued a strategic consensus concept focusing on the Persian Gulf. Secretary of State Alexander Haig set out in April 1981 on a tour of the key Gulf states to urge support for a U.S. presence in the area as part of a unified stand against the common enemy, the Soviet Union. To his chagrin, he discovered that Saudi Arabia, in particular, saw Israel — not the USSR — as the immediate threat to stability in the area, and that all the Arab states he consulted were reluctant to work openly in concert with the United States as long as the Palestinian issue was unresolved. Whether or not this was an Arab dodge to avoid responding to U.S. pressure for a military presence on Arab soil, it is a repeatedly stated policy which makes it necessary that America address the Palestinian problem.

The Options Today

In view of the many inter-Arab and other intraregional disputes, it is highly doubtful that a strategic consensus would develop even if the Palestinian problem were resolved. But as long as there are no discernible signs of progress toward such a resolution, the Arab world has a safe excuse for not participating in America's plans.

Considering this Arab position, most observers view the Haig strategic consensus concept as practically a dead letter, reduced to little more than buying friendship with sales of highly sophisticated weapons. And even that has failed to produce real friendship in terms of support for U.S. interests and movement towards peace with Israel — as the post-AWACS Saudi Arabian stance reveals fully. It should be noted, however, that Morocco, Egypt, Oman, the Sudan and non-Arab Turkey have welcomed increasing bilateral defense cooperation with the U.S. despite the absence of a strategic consensus or of a solution of the Palestinian problem.

American officials are debating whether to give priority to continued military arms sales to countries like Jordan and Saudi Arabia for whatever gains this may bring, or to attempt to resolve the Palestinian issue on the highly speculative prospect that its resolution will yield support for a pro-American Arab alliance in the Middle East.

Neither approach augurs well for Israel, which is already

registering alarm at the sale of ultra-sophisticated arms to Saudi Arabia, soon to Jordan, and possibly to Iraq. Resolution of the Palestinian issue in order to buy Arab friendship and support would clearly mean intolerable pressures on Israel, and it would resist them vehemently. Likewise, a comprehensive approach to peace seems unattainable at this time in light of Syria's unremitting hostility toward Israel, coupled with its internal distress and its inability to calm the Lebanese situation. Moreover, Jordan has withdrawn from the peace process and has chosen to support Iraq in the Iran-Iraq war, a step hardly conducive to stability and rapprochement with Israel.

Given this conjuncture of circumstances, few avenues remain open to the United States. Yet, it should not be overlooked that the Palestinian problem, whether one views it as the key to Arab friendship or as the central item in any comprehensive peace plan, is still a real dilemma for both Israel and the Palestinians, a human problem which merits resolution for its own sake. Those who resist the Begin government's current trend toward encouraging new Jewish settlements in the West Bank fear it will lead — if it has not already led — to Israel's total "colonization" of the area, and argue that an active and energetic U.S. policy in favor of successful autonomy negotiations is necessary.

The Secretary of State has named a special representative to the autonomy talks — a yet untried Assistant Secretary, Richard Fairbanks — to report to him rather than to the President. This was done after Haig's hasty visit to both Egypt and Israel, where he discovered he could not exercise a "quick fix" on the unresolved issues surrounding autonomy. Clearly, all parties intended to keep the talks alive at least until the completion of Israel's withdrawal from the last third of the Sinai. It appears plain that unless the United States is prepared to continue its pressure on both Israel and Egypt — and especially on Egypt which now has little incentive to continue the talks — they will falter and leave no realistic prospect for any kind of Palestinian self-governance in the immediate future.

Moreover, the ominous situation in Southern Lebanon, where the PLO has massed a sizable force, added to civil deterioration in Syria which may oblige that country to pull its troops out of Lebanon and thus throw that unhappy fragmented nation into another round of civil wars, bodes ill for stability, indeed for peace, in the Middle East. Israel will have little interest in dealing with Palestinian autonomy if it faces military threats from within Lebanon. And Syria's missiles there have yet to be removed, despite U.S. mediation through Ambassador Philip Habib.

In sum, the United States options are rapidly diminishing. The strategic consensus focusing on the Persian Gulf states seems all but dead. Israel's participation in the defense of the Gulf area has strained credulity even in Israel, where the Labor opposition almost won a vote of no-confidence on the ill-fated strategic cooperation agreement between Washington and Jerusalem. And the agreement fell by the wayside after Israel had effectively annexed the Golan Heights without any consultation or advance notice to its American protector. The Lebanese situation is deteriorating rapidly to a flash point of real danger. President Hafez al-Assad of Syria is faced with open rebellion from Sunni Muslim extremists. Egypt is already looking toward some reintegration into the Arab world. How, under these circumstances, can the United States expect to advance the cause of Palestinian autonomy?

The United States has a real interest in trying to advance that cause, even when it is clear to everyone that its resolution, even on the most successful terms, will not ameliorate the manifold problems of the region. The persistence of the Palestinian issue undermines the Arab moderates, plays into Soviet hands, and poses difficult moral and practical problems for Israelis who fear the long-term effects of the occupation or the absorption of so many Arabs into Israel. It may well be that no solution is possible in the near future. But the United States must not forsake a sustained effort to get the parties to talk to each other, principally Jordan, the Palestinians of the West Bank and Gaza, and Israel. Indeed, the United States has no choice but to persist, lest the Palestinian problem continue to fester and, in the end, present Israel with its most fearsome dilemma: an occupation that grows harsher with the passing years, increasing hostility of the younger Palestinians, and the end of all hope of reconciliation between the peoples on the two sides of the Jordan River.

But, as French President François Mitterrand, a firm advocate both of Palestinian self-determination and of continued secure existence for Israel, has pointed out, if this reconciliation is to occur, there must first be a fundamental change in the PLO's Covenant and ideology. To date, no such change has been discerned, despite France's wishful search for signs of an altered PLO policy, and despite frequent urgings by third parties that the PLO alter it. Until there is at least some positive move which indicates a true acceptance of the State of Israel in the Middle East, real progress on the Palestinian issue is not likely.

Note

1. The specific language of the resolution called for "Termination of all claims or states of belligerency and respect for and acknowledgment of the sovereignty, territorial integrity and political independence of every State in the area and their right to live in peace within secure and recognized boundaries free from threats or acts of force..."

CONTRIBUTORS

Daniel J. Elazar received his doctorate in political science from the University of Chicago. He is Professor of Political Studies and head of the Institute of Local Government at Bar-Ilan University in Israel, president of the Jerusalem Institute for Federal Studies, chairman of the Center for Jewish Community Studies (Jerusalem and Philadelphia), and senior fellow of the Center for the Study of Federalism at Temple University.

Galia Golan received her Ph.D. from the Hebrew University of Jerusalem, where she teaches political science and Russian studies, and is former director of the University's Soviet and Eastern European Research Center. After studies at Brandeis, the University of Geneva and the Sorbonne, she worked as an Eastern European specialist for the U.S. Government before emigrating to Israel in 1966. Her most recent book, *The Soviet Union and the PLO: Uneasy Alliance,* was published by Praeger in 1980.

George E. Gruen,Ph.D. from Columbia University in international relations and law, wrote his dissertation on *Turkey, Israel and the Palestine Question.* He has taught international relations and Middle East politics at Columbia and the City and Brooklyn Colleges of The City University of New York. He is director of Middle East Affairs at the American Jewish Committee and an associate in the Columbia University Seminar on the Middle East. His articles on "The United States, Israel and the Middle East" appear in the *American Jewish Year Book.*

Yehoshafat Harkabi has M.A. degrees in public administration from Harvard and in philosophy and Arabic literature from the

Hebrew University. He was an Israeli delegate to the 1949 Rhodes Armistice Negotiations and served as deputy chief (1950-55) and then chief (1955-59) of Military Intelligence of the Israel Defence Forces. M. Hexter Professor of International Relations and Middle Eastern Studies at the Hebrew University, he is the author of numerous works on the Arab-Israeli conflict.

Rita E. Hauser holds a Ph.D. in political economy from the University of Strasbourg and an LL.B. from Harvard and from New York University. She was the United States Representative to the United Nations Commission on Human Rights, and is now a senior partner in the law firm of Stroock & Stroock & Lavan. She is a vice president of the American Jewish Committee and chairman of its Foreign Affairs Commission.